Jacob of Sarug's Homily on Samson

Texts from Christian Late Antiquity

63

Series Editor

George Anton Kiraz

TeCLA (Texts from Christian Late Antiquity) is a series presenting ancient Christian texts both in their original languages and with accompanying contemporary English translations.

Jacob of Sarug's Homily on Samson

Translated by

Dana Miller

Edited with Notes and Introduction by

✝ Mary T. Hansbury

2021

Gorgias Press LLC, 954 River Road, Piscataway, NJ, 08854, USA

www.gorgiaspress.com

Copyright © 2021 by Gorgias Press LLC

All rights reserved under International and Pan-American Copyright Conventions. No part of this publication may be reproduced, stored in a retrieval system or transmitted in any form or by any means, electronic, mechanical, photocopying, recording, scanning or otherwise without the prior written permission of Gorgias Press LLC.

2021

ISBN 978-1-4632-4290-9   ISSN 1935-6846

Library of Congress Cataloging-in-Publication Data

A Cataloging-in-Publication Record is available from the Library of Congress.

Printed in the United States of America

Table of Contents

Table of Contents v
Introduction 1
   Outline 1
   Summary 7
Text and Translation 9
   Thy Mysteries are revealed from the readings 10
   Samson rich in parables and mysteries 14
   The righteous, rich in the revelation of the Divinity 16
   …Samson, who went into the land of the Philistines…our Lord, who came to espouse the daughter of the pagans 20
   A comb of honey appeared in the lion, a great parable which could not be interpreted save in our Lord 26
   Samson: beautiful; odious; defiled 30
   Samson and the foxes 32
   Samson sets the region on fire 36
   Samson thirsts and the Lord provides 38
   Samson and the harlot 40
   Sheol: the Lord; Samson 42
   Samson enabled by the mysteries of his Lord 46
   Samson and Delilah 48
   Samson to be a mirror 54
   Samson shaven, blinded and made a laughing stock unto the Philistines 56
   God heard Samson's prayer of contrition and granted his request 60
Bibliography of Works Cited 65

Index 69
   Biblical References 69
   Index of Names 69

INTRODUCTION

INFORMATION ON THIS HOMILY
Homily Title: On Samson
Source of Text: *Homiliae Selectae Mar-Jacob Sarugensis*, edited by Paul Bedjan (Paris-Leipzig: Harrassowitz, 1910), 2nd ed. Piscataway: Gorgias Press, 2006), vol. 5, pp. 331–355. [Homily 160]

OUTLINE

Jacob of Serugh was born *circa* 451 in Curtam, a town on the Euphrates in Mesopotamia. His father was a priest of the village. He received his education at the School of Edessa and was there around 470, when the writings of Theodore of Mopsuestia would have been available in Syriac. However, he lived a quiet life of prayer and avoided the theological controversies following the Council of Chalcedon, which was held in the year he was born. His appointment as *Chorepiscopos* at Hawra is a clear sign of his talents in preaching and spiritual guidance. He served in this capacity until 518 when he was consecrated Bishop of Batnan, not far from Edessa, in the district of Serugh. Mar Jacob died 29 November 521. Both the Syrian Orthodox and Maronite Churches venerate him as a saint.

Jacob is one of the great poets of the early Syriac tradition. St. Ephrem (d.373), with the depth of his insights and his originality, can astound and even bewilder his readers, whereas Jacob is more straightforward – beautiful, but ever concerned about pastoral care and the edification of the Christian faithful. He developed this approach as he lived at a time of doctrinal conflict, which he chose to avoid. Rather he focused on Scripture and the history of Salvation.

Jacob's thinking is essentially symbolic; like Ephrem's it shuns the logic and precision of Greek thought. Perhaps for this reason Jacob has been misunderstood and even considered as purely mythological. Fortunately, a re-evaluation in recent years has allowed his true thinking to emerge.[1]

None of the early Syriac writers give a systematic treatise on their symbolic thinking. Neusner writes that in the 5th and 6th centuries "a mode of talking about God took shape, both in synagogue art and in rabbinic writings, that appealed not to propositions but to symbolic modes of discourse." And that the Babylonian Talmudic and Midrashic compilations undertook to express thought in not only propositional but also symbolic discourse. One might consult his book with profit. What he discusses occurs during the lifetime of Mar Jacob.[2]

Brock writes of the 4th cent. as the end of Jewish traditions being employed by Syriac authors.[3]

In a subsequent article Becker suggests, commenting on Brock's article: "If movement of material came to an end how to explain Syriac anti-Jewish literature?" Becker does not feel Syriac material will revolutionize but shed light.[4] Might the same not be said about symbolism in Judaism shedding light on symbolism in Syriac writings: not influence but parallel developments, not derivation but symbiosis.

Kollamparampil has well noted the idea of divine pedagogy in the thought of Jacob. "Hence all events and developments described in the Scriptures as history of salvation are interrelated and issue out of a single teaching running through the Old and New Testaments. It is this interrelationship that gives coherence and edifying enlightenment to the typological vision of Jacob of Serugh.

---

[1] See the comments of A. Golitzin, "The Image and Glory of God in Jacob of Serug's Homily, *On the Chariot that Ezekiel the Prophet Saw*," *St. Vladimir's Theological Quarterly* 47 (2003), 323–64, esp. 323–30.

[2] See J. Neusner, *Symbol and Theology in Early Judaism* (Minneapolis, 1991), xiv–xv.

[3] See S.P. Brock, "Jewish traditions in Syriac sources", *Journal of Jewish Studies* 30 (1979), 212–32 (reprinted in *Studies in Syriac Christianity*, 1992, chapter IV).

[4] See A.M. Becker, "Polishing the mirror: some thoughts on Syriac sources and early Judaism", in *Envisioning Judaism: Studies in Honor of Peter Schäfer* (Tübingen, 2013), 897–915.

Divine providence, rich in discernment, is the guiding factor behind the divine economy."[5]

Konat makes an important distinction of how the prophets pictured types by foreseeing Christ. "This is a very prominent concept in Jacob's mind. It is true that he says at times that Christ came to fulfill the Old Testament. But most of the time he emphasizes more specifically that Christ did not follow the prophecy, but rather the prophets foresaw the coming of Christ and his acts of salvation and prophesied accordingly."[6]

Prophecies make known the Only-Begotten through types and symbols. These types and symbols contain the whole truth about the Son and are recorded in the Old Testament. Rather than openly revealing him these prophecies point to him. This means that God manifested his Beloved through the Old Testament. Yet he had covered it as if with a veil to camouflage the coming of his Son.[7] As Jacob said:

> This is what the veil on Moses' face symbolizes:
> that the words of prophecy are veiled;
> the Lord covered Moses' face for this reason,
> that it might be a type for prophecy, which is also veiled.
> The Father kept the Son in concealment, without anyone being aware,
> but He wished to reveal this matter to the world in symbolic terms;
> He wished to speak about His Beloved One through prophecy
> and so covered up Moses to make him a figure for prophecy
> so that, whenever a prophet arose on earth to speak, it might be recognized
> that his words were veiled from those from those who heard them,

---

[5] T. Kollamparampil, Jacob of Serugh: Select Festal Homilies, p. 21.

[6] J. Konat, "Typological Exegesis in the Metrical Homilies of Jacob of Serugh," *Parole de l'Orient* 31 (2006) 109–121.

[7] See A. Elkhoury, "Jesus Christ, the Eye of Prophecy", in *Patrimoine syriaque: Les exégètes syriaques. Actes du Colloque* 13 (2015), p. 3.

> that there was something hidden, concealed in the matter of which he spoke,
> and for his words to be understood, it requires an awareness of what they symbolize.[8]

In the Hebrew Bible the book of Judges is a prophetical work. It belongs to the second of the three main divisions of that Bible, the Prophets, consisting of the Former Prophets; Isaiah, Jeremiah, Ezekiel; and the Book of the Twelve. The Former Prophets include Joshua, Judges, Samuel and Kings. Therefore one finds in the book of Judges not historical records but prophetical teaching and, as in the other prophetical works, the use of history to illustrate and reveal the character and work of Israel's God.

See Judges 13–16 for the account of Samson:
Ch. 13 The call of Samson
Ch. 14 Samson's marriage feast
Ch.15 Samson's revenge
Ch. 16 Samson and Delilah

Some of the historical/prophetic interplay can be found in Jacob of Serug's reading of Samson's marriage feast (Judges 14): the story of Samson and the Timnite woman foreshadowing Christ betrothed to the Church.

> But a mystery encountered him there, one manifest and clear.
> So as to espouse a wife he descended to the region of the Philistines,
> but a lion's whelp roared against him like a mighty foe.
> Who does Samson resemble if not our Lord, who came to espouse
> the Church of the Nations, but death encountered Him like a valiant adversary?
> Samson went down to take that daughter of the gentiles,
> hereby depicting our Lord who betrothed the daughter of the pagans by His Gospel.[9]

---

[8] S.P. Brock, ["Jacob of Serugh on the Veil of Moses", *Sobornost/Eastern Churches Review* 3:1 (1981), pp. 70-85.] *Jacob of Serugh, Homily on the Veil of Moses* (Piscataway, NJ, 2009), lines 21–33.

Mar Jacob says Samson went to the land of Philistines without armour and tore his enemies with the armour of mysteries:

> The mysteries of his Lord shone brilliantly in him like luminaries,
> and they bestowed on him power and strength to slay the lion.
> Without armour, without a sword, he rent it with his hands,
> for the youth carried mysteries as weapons on the path that he took.[10]

Elkhoury emphasizes that Mar Jacob identifies this Bride with the Church of the Nations. She is the Daughter of the pagans whom the daughter of the uncircumcised, i.e. the Timnite woman, typifies.[11] He also comments on the lion charging Samson as a symbol of death befalling Jesus and Samson's defeat of the lion depicting God's killing death to save His Bride from its grip.

> To betroth a woman, who depicts a type of the Church of light,
> Samson was led and, for this reason, he killed the lion's whelp.
> The daughter of the Pagans typified the Daughter of the Uncircumscribed,
> for the Son of God killed death as He saved her.[12]

Mar Jacob's exegetical method is closely linked with his approach to the divine mystery and his symbolic theology. As a necessary condition for receiving the true and deeper meaning of Scripture, he requires love, the soul's inclination to God and its abandoning earthly things.[13] Faith as indicated by Ephrem is never neglected. But there is in Jacob's *Letters* and *Mimre* an insistence on the power of love as an exegetical principle. It does not seem to be formulaic

---

[9] Homily on Samson, lines 80–86.

[10] Homily on Samson, lines 103–106.

[11] A. Elkhoury, *Types and Symbols of the Church in the Writings of Jacob of Sarug* (Dissertation: Katholische Universität Eichstätt-Ingolstadt, 2017), 290.

[12] Homily on Samuel, lines, 107–110.

[13] See Hansbury, "Love as an Exegetical Principle in Jacob of Serug," vol. 27 (2011) *The Harp*, 353–68.

or even only an aspect of cognition. Rather it is intrinsic to his Soteriology which underlies his understanding of Scripture. According to Boulos Sony, the Christological controversies of his time pushed Jacob deeper into Scripture, where instead of definitions, he found the mystery (*râzâ*) of Christ on every page.[14] According to Mar Jacob, the Scriptures provide the God-experience of the people of God in various forms of human communications. "Rather than providing defined truths the Scriptures furnish experiences of divine-human encounters."[15] Thus Scripture is an ongoing revelation, through its mysteries, of God's love for mankind and the only adequate and effective exegetical response according to Mar Jacob is love (*ḥûbâ*).

> Scripture enlightens the soul's eyes through study.
> Read, discerning one, and fill up with light from it through
>   Love (*ḥûbâ*).
> The Sun shines from divine Scriptural readings
> upon the minds of those who encounter them with discernment.
> Like lamps of a great light within the darkness
> God put Scriptures into the World so that it would be enlightened by them.
> The soul of the one who loves them is enlightened by scriptural readings
> and, possessing them, he walks as if in the great light of day.
> Draw near to Scripture, lovingly, and see its beauty,
> for without Love (*ḥûbâ*) it does not allow you to see its face.
> If you read without Love (*ḥûbâ*) you do not benefit,
> for Love (*ḥubâ*) is the gate through which one enters into understanding.
> Thus Scripture demands of you, when you have taken it up,

---

[14] B Sony, "La méthode exégétique de Jacques de Saroug", *Parole de l'Orient* 9 (1979/1980), pp. 67–103.

[15] T. Kollamparampil, *Jacob of Serugh: Select Festal Homilies* (Rome/Bangalore, 1997), 26

not to read it unless you love it more than yourself.[16]

Summary

I. Thy mysteries are revealed from the readings (12–24)

II. Samson rich in parables and mysteries (25–54)

III. The righteous, rich in the revelations of the Divinity (55–86)

IV. …Samson, who went into the land of the Philistines…our Lord, who came to espouse the daughter of the pagans (87–126)

V. A comb of honey appeared in the lion, a great parable which could not be interpreted save in our Lord (127–170)

VI. Samson: beautiful; odious; defiled (171–200)

VII Samson and the foxes (201–226)

VIII Samson sets the region on fire (227–254)

IX Samson thirsts and the Lord provides (255–270)

X Samson and the harlot (271–294)

XI Sheol: the Lord; Samson (295–320)

XII Samson enabled by the mysteries of his Lord (327–352)

XIII Samson and Delilah (353–413)

XIV Samson to be a mirror (413–442)

XV Samson shaven, blinded and made a laughingstock unto the Philistines (443–468)

XVI God heard Samson's prayer of contrition and granted his request (469–486)

---

[16] "On Elisha and on the King of Moab" in Jacob of Serug's Homilies on Elisha, tr. and Introd. S.A. Kaufman (Gorgias Press, 2010), 1–14.

TEXT AND TRANSLATION

HOMILY 160: A HOMILY ON SAMSON

THY MYSTERIES ARE REVEALED FROM THE READINGS

The sunrise of Your mysteries reveals itself from amidst the readings:
O Son of God, open for me my eyes that I may behold its beauty!
Your great image is borne by the books of prophecy
and they solemnly raise You up, so that the world might see how beautiful You are.

5 From generation to generation Your mystery has luminously appeared,
and by its sunrise it has gladdened the one who sees and marvels at You.
By the parables and the dark sayings found in the Scriptures
In diverse places the just have depicted You through their revelations.
Together with their times and their generations they solemnly bore You up,

10 and one handed You over to another, so that in You they might be renowned.
The righteous Noah received You from Seth, that goodly man,
and through the descendance of the world he placed You with Abraham.
Isaac received You and raised up Your image on Golgotha;[1]
Jacob stole Your image and fled to the land of Adam.[2]

---

[1] Gen. 28:18.

[2] I.e., Mesopotamia.

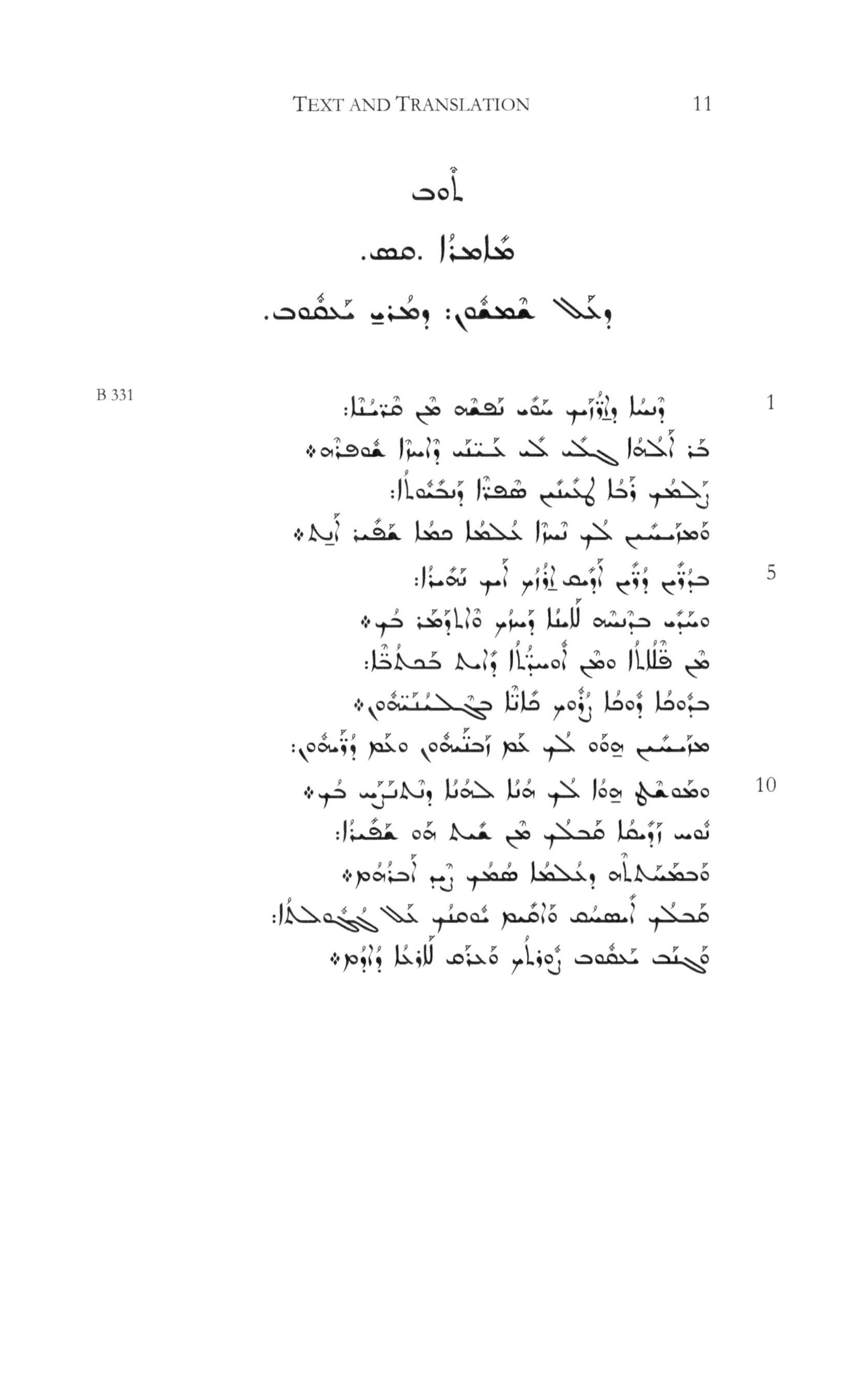

B 331

15 You laid Your testimony on Joseph, who became illustrious in Egypt,[3]
and Moses saw You on the Mount of Sinai with Your Begetter.
Aaron depicted[4] You by the blood of sacrifices and offerings,
and the entire path of the great slaughter[5] he sprinkled with blood.
Joshua, the son of Nun, was arrayed with Your beautiful name,
20 He who at his will held back the day so that it would not wane.[6]
Gideon sketched You with the dew that he brought down by his entreaty,[7]
and by You he utterly defeated the camp of the Midianites.[8]
Jephthah prepared the path of Your sufferings by the slaying of his daughter,[9]
and he sprinkled it with the virgin's blood on Your account.

---

[3] Psalm 80:5 in the LXX.

[4] Depict (*sûr*): here there are 4 uses of depiction, l.17, 32, 86, 107. Each points to a visual image. Depict is used to represent or signify which has a prophetic dimension. Aaron depicted the Son of God with the blood of sacrifices, l.17. Samson depicts our Lord, l.86. And the woman to be espoused depicts, l.107. Actually in l.31 Jacob asks to depict personally! Jacob like Ephrem speaks of types and symbols (*râzê*) as being depicted or drawn in Scripture. In Ephrem: "God or Christ is the artist who in the Scriptures has painted pictures of the whole economy of salvation in the words and deeds of the prophets and the apostles," see S.H. Griffith, "The image of the image-maker in the poetry of Ephraem the Syrian", *Studia Patristica* 25 (1993), 258–69.

[5] I.e., the crucifixion.

[6] Lit., 'move forward', Josh. 10:12.

[7] Judg. 6:36–40.

[8] Judg. 7:1.

[9] Judg. 11:34–39.

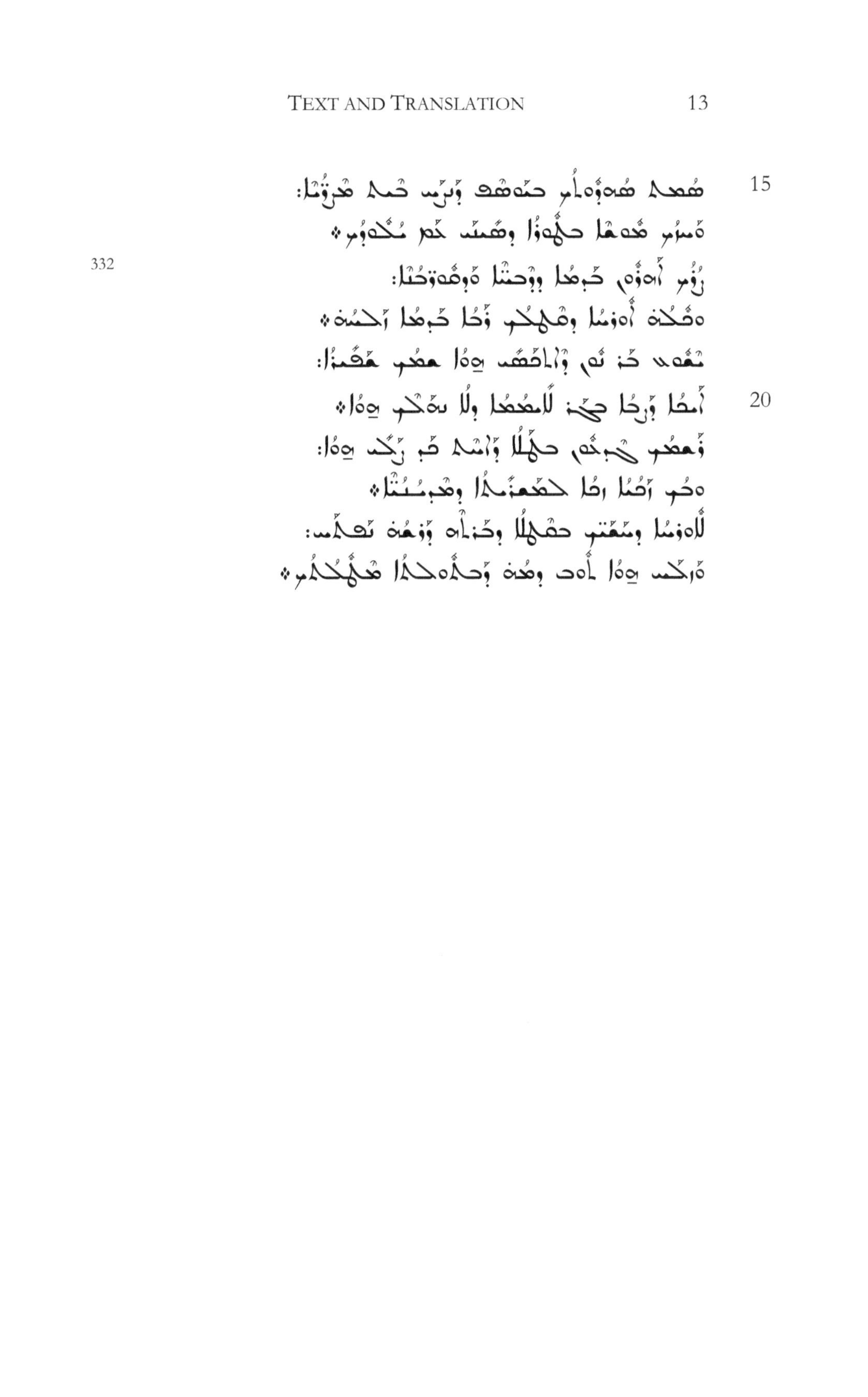

SAMSON RICH IN PARABLES AND MYSTERIES

25 But what should I say of Samson, for he also was illustrious,
and he is rich in parables and mysteries for whoever examines him.[10]
Behold, a homily on the glorious demands of me that I also
write down his history together with these other valiant and famous men.
The place of his figure is empty, belittled, and is painful to me,
30 since I have not fashioned for him the figure of a homily with the virtuous.
Grant me, 0 Lord, that I may repay my debt also to this Nazirite,
that I may depict also for him a beautiful likeness full of wonder!
It is not because he did foolish deeds on various occasions
that I should disdain and neglect this man, who is recorded with the illustrious.
35 The elect Paul sings unto the man who possesses understanding,
'Time would fail me to speak of Samson'.[11]
Time, therefore, would fail me also to speak
Of this Nazirite and of the allegories found in him.
It was, indeed, his lot also from God that
40 in his time he should be a saviour for Israel, as it is said.[12]
Because of his faith in God, he was among the renowned,
and among the Judges he was most skilled during his own day.
The mother of this man beheld an angel who spoke with her,
and announced to her that she would conceive and bear a Nazirite and a saviour.

---

[10] I.e., his history.
[11] Cf., Heb. 11:32.
[12] Judg. 13:5.

TEXT AND TRANSLATION   15

45 That wise woman told her husband
of the revelation that she had had from God,
Then once more the man of God appeared to her and to her husband,
repeating his words to the woman that she would conceive and give birth to Samson.[13]
He enjoined the woman that she should not drink wine or strong liquor,
50 nor should she eat any sort of fruit of the vine.[14]
"The child will be a Nazirite unto the Lord all the days of his life," he said,[15]
"and his mother shall rear him without defilement."[16]
The woman's husband made a meal and placed it on a stone,
then sacrificial fire manifested itself upon the offering.[17]

THE RIGHTEOUS, RICH IN THE REVELATION OF THE DIVINITY

55 Nowadays we should marvel at the righteous men of those times,
how clear-minded they were, how simple and bereft of guile.
They spoke face to face with angels,
they were rich in the revelations of the Divinity;
they were humble, innocent and straight-forward

---

[13] Judg. 13:9ff.
[14] Judg. 13:14.
[15] Cf., Judg. 13:7.
[16] Cf., Judg. 13:14.
[17] Judg. 13:20.

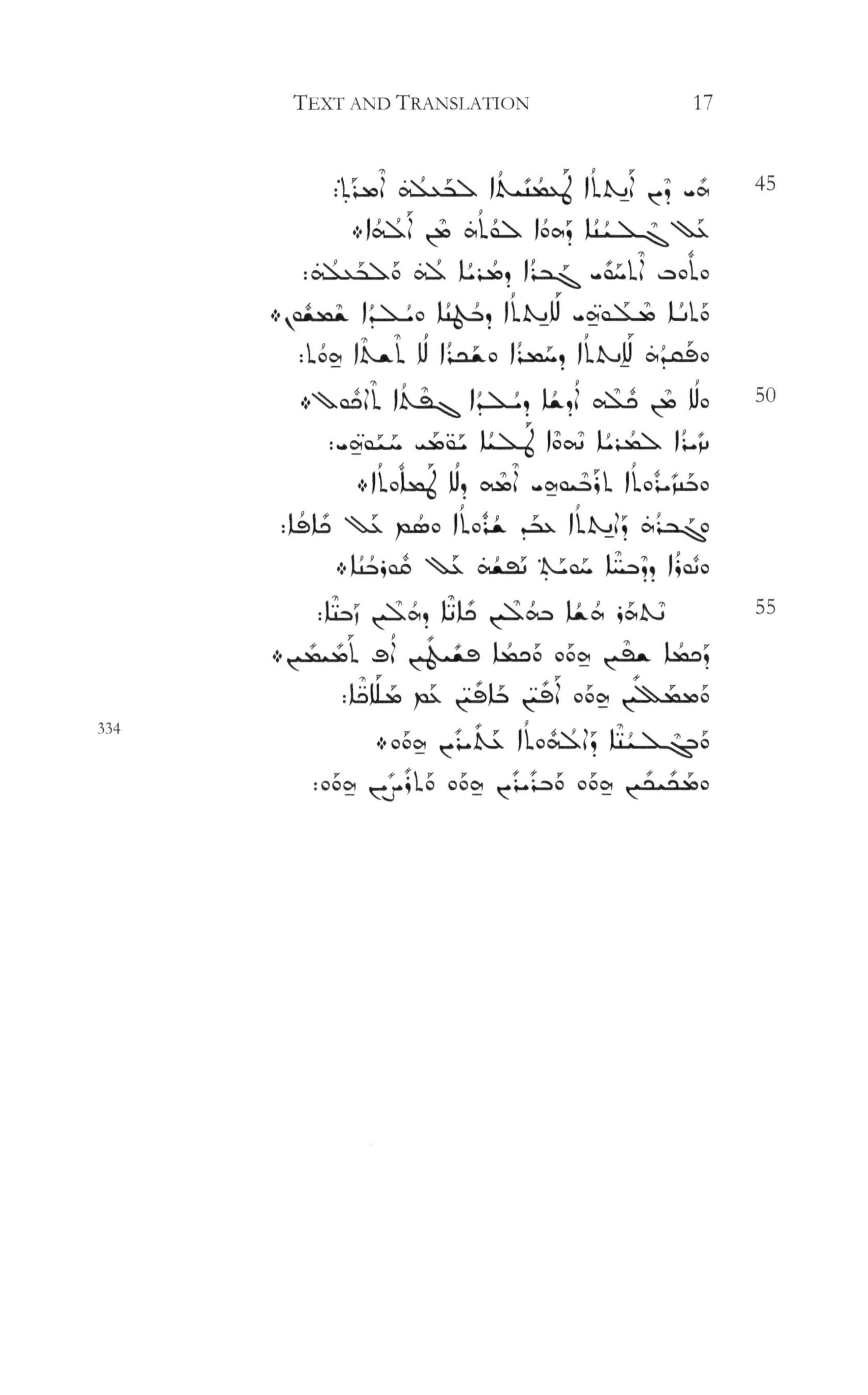

60	and they did not become proud or puffed up by their revelations.
	Like a native, like a countryman, like a neighbor,
	the watcher[18] spoke to Manoah and his wife concerning Samson,
	and in such a manner did they accept what he told them;
	Innocently they spoke with him, fearing nothing.
65	In their simplicity they even made a meal for him,
	but the sacrificial flame devoured it.
	The flame rose up, and as the angel was fiery also,
	he ascended in the fire which devoured Manoah's offering.[19]
	The man of fire and the flame ascended to Heaven,
70	and there was great wonder in the revelation that there came to pass.
	As He had promised, God gave the barren woman a son,
	Samson, who was to become a saviour for his enslaved people.
	The Lord gave him power and strength and bravery,
	So as to take up arms and deliver the downtrodden nation.
75	The Lord chose him and sent him to wage war against the Philistines;
	He gave him strength so as vigorously to massacre them.
	Samson began to visit the villages of the Philistines,
	for the power of God had begun to triumph through him.
	He went down to that region because of the woman he desired to take,

---

[18] The Syriac tradition frequently designates angels as Watchers (Dan. 4:13–17). Watchers figure prominently in pseudepigraphic and later Jewish mystical literature. In Merkabah texts such as 3 Enoch, they are a separate order: "Above all these are four great princes called Watchers…their abode is opposite the throne of Glory…they receive glory from the glory of the Almighty and are praised with the praise." See 3 Enoch 28:1–3. Angels are the central theme of 3 Enoch. See P. Schäfer, *The Hidden and the Manifest. Some Major Themes in Early Jewish Mysticism* (Albany, 1992), 123–161.

[19] Judg. 13:20.

Text and Translation

80	but a mystery encountered him there, one manifest and clear.
	So as to espouse a wife he descended to the region of the Philistines,
	but a lion's whelp roared against him like a mighty foe.[20]
	Who does Samson resemble if not our Lord, who came to espouse the Church of the Nations, but death encountered Him like a valiant adversary?
85	Samson went down to take that daughter of the gentiles,
	hereby depicting our Lord who betrothed the daughter of the pagans[21] by His Gospel.

…SAMSON, WHO WENT INTO THE LAND OF THE PHILISTINES…OUR LORD, WHO CAME TO ESPOUSE THE DAUGHTER OF THE PAGANS

	Come and look here, if you know how to see well,
	and take, depict an image of these virgins and their betrothed!
	Against Samson, who went into the lands of the Philistines,
90	A lion's whelp came forth menacingly to make him a mockery.
	And against our Lord, who came to espouse the daughter of the pagans,[22]
	death made bold to come, to bring Him into his lair and to bear down on Him.
	Let us now see what was done to death and to the lion
	by our Lord and also by Samson, who was a Nazirite unto Him.
95	The manslayer[23] sent a lion against Samson
	because he saw in him a comely form replete with beauty.
	The beauty of that Hebrew he sought to ravage
	by means of the lion which came forth and encountered the young Samson.
	Then the Son's mystery dawned upon that Nazirite

---

[20] Judg. 14: 5.

[21] "Daughter of the pagans," "daughter of the nations," are images of the Church. Mar Jacob interprets Samson's journey to marry the Philistine woman as resembling Christ's journey to marry the Church.

[22] Lit., 'of the Arameans'.

[23] I.e., the devil. See John 8:44.

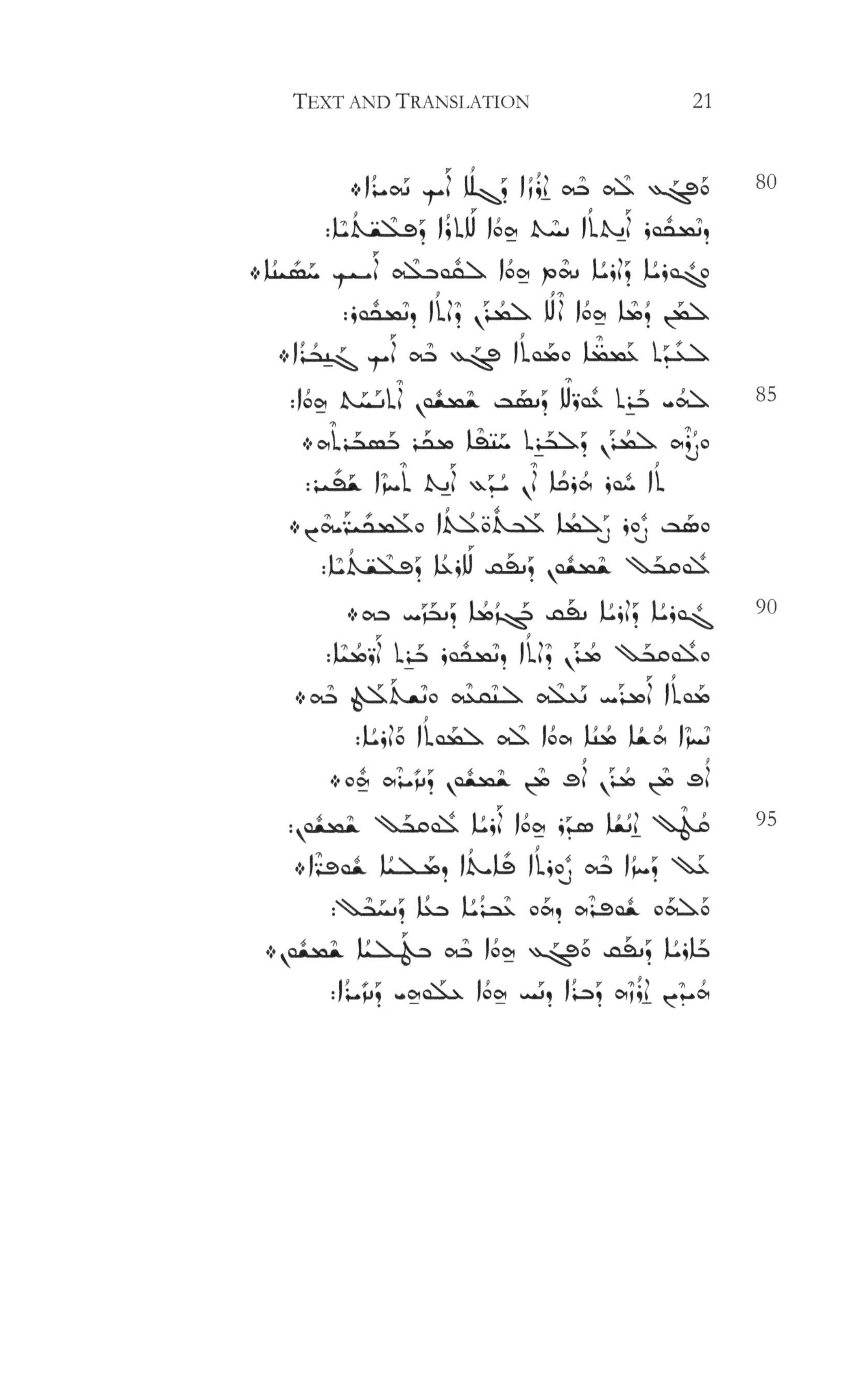

100 and gave him power so as to depict an image full of wonder.
Then the Spirit of the Lord mightily took possession of him,[24]
and he seized the lion's whelp and tore it asunder like a kid.[25]
The mysteries[26] of his Lord shone brilliantly in him like luminaries,
and they bestowed on him power and strength to slay the lion.
105 Without armour, without a sword, he rent it with his hands,
for the youth carried mysteries as weapons on the path that he took.
To espouse a woman, who depicts the type of the Church of light,
Samson made his way, and for her sake he slew the lion's whelp.
The Daughter of the gentiles was typified by the daughter of the pagans,
110 for the Son of God slew death when He saved her.
He raised up an image of our Lord in the land of the Philistines,
for it was Samson's lot to raise it up there.
The Son of God moved from His place[27] and came to our land
to espouse the Church of the Nations,[28] as we have said.

---

[24] Cf. Judg. 14:6.

[25] Cf., Judg. 14:6.

[26] Or, 'types' (*râzê*).

[27] Place (*atrâ*): Golitzen analyzes its occurrence in Aphrahat also giving its linguistic history, including roots of *maqom* in the Hebrew Bible, as the place of divine manifestation and *topos* in the Septuagint, and as "a stand in for God himself." In the Hekhalot literature, *maqom* is used as divine name. See A. Golitzin, "The Place of the Presence of God: Aphrahat of Persia's portrait of the Christian Holy Man", in *Sunaxias Eucharistias: Studies in Honor of Archimandrite Aimilianos of Simonos Petras* (Athens, 2003), 391–447.

[28] God's rejection of Israel, the Nation, and the election of Nations in its place is a predominant theme of anti-Jewish polemics in Syriac writers. Hence the ecclesiological figure of the betrothal of Christ, the Bridegroom to the Bride, the Church of the Nations. See R. Murray, *Symbols of Church and Kingdom* (repr. Piscataway, 2004), 41–68. And see S.K. Joshua, *Church as the Bride of Christ. Ecclesiological and Societal Understanding of the Early Syriac Church based on Select Homilies of Mar Jacob of Serugh* (Christian Heritage Rediscovered 77; Delhi, 2020), 287.

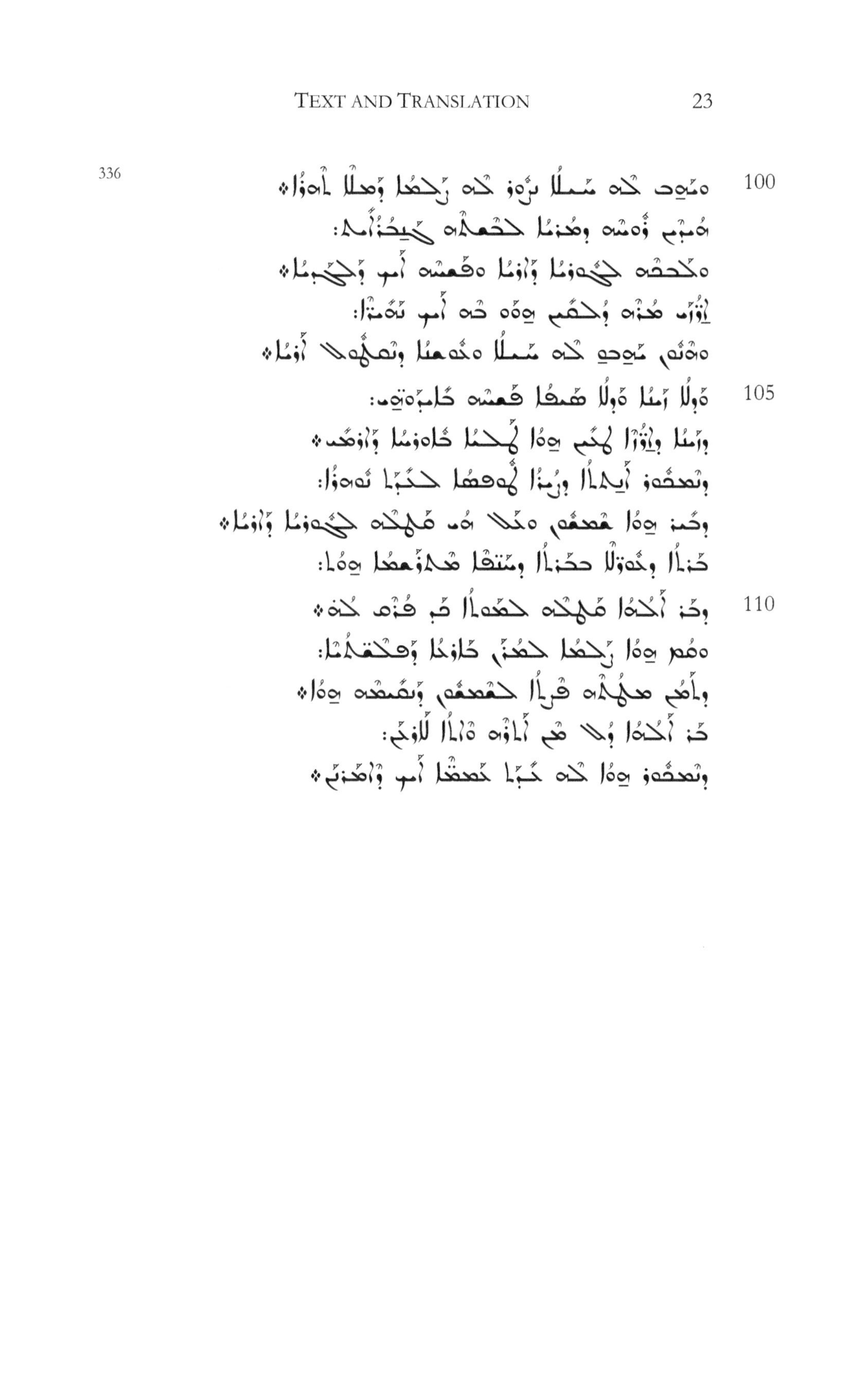

115	But death encountered Him, the ravening lion that devoured all the generations,
and He slew death as Samson slew that lion.[29]
He continued His way and by His Cross He betrothed and took
her for whom He had descended to the home of terrestrial beings.
The lion was unable to stop the path of Samson,
120	for he espoused and took a wife as he pleased and only then did he depart.
Nor, indeed, did death put a stop to the path[30] of the Son of God,
for He took the Church, made her His own, and only then did He ascend.
These mysteries shone forth brilliantly in this Hebrew man,
and for this reason he prospered and slew the lion, as you have heard.
125	He rent the lion asunder, went his way and espoused the woman as he desired;
he turned to go and the mystery was clearly set forth in him.

---

[29] "The lion which met Samson was the type of death that met Christ. Samson could kill the lion without any weapons because he operated as a type of Christ. Our author affirms that it was nothing but the mysteries of the Son which gave Samson such immense might. The event was a figure of the unlimited power of the Son who conquered death. The animal could never have stopped Samson from continuing on his way, just as death too had no power to interfere with the way of Christ." See J.A. Konat, The Old Testament Types of Christ as reflected in the Select Metrical Homilies (memre) of Jacob of Serugh (Dissertation, Louvain-la-Neuve, 1998), 90; cf. also his "Typological exegesis in the metrical homilies of Jacob of Serugh", *Parole de l'Orient* 31 (2006), 109–21.

[30] On the image of the 'path' or 'way' (*ûrḥâ*), see T. Kollamparampil, "Divine pedagogy on the road of salvation and early Syriac perspectives", *Parole de l'Orient* 36 (2011), 85–98. On this path (p. 87), "Adam is an image of the invisible Only-Begotten, and when he attains his goal, he attains the full likeness of the Only Begotten…Adam's growth to perfection in, through and with Christ, is the foundation of this imagery of 'the way' that depicts the stages of revelation, the patterns of human behavior, the story of salvation…in a symbolic manner." See also F. Rilliet, "La métaphore du chemin dans la sotériologie de Jacques de Saroug", *Studia Patristica* 85 (1993), 324–31.

TEXT AND TRANSLATION   25

A COMB OF HONEY APPEARED IN THE LION, A GREAT PARABLE WHICH COULD NOT BE INTERPRETED SAVE IN OUR LORD

A comb of honey appeared in the lion,[31]
A great parable which could not be interpreted save in our Lord.
Samson ate of the honey and ate from the skeleton;
130   this was a new deed, even that the edible proceeded from the eater.[32]
The revelation came upon the Nazirite and gave him light,
And with allegories and hidden types his path proceeded swiftly.
He seized upon a parable, that sweet came forth from the bitter,[33]
And except in our Lord, the saying that he propounded could not be explained.
135   He composed a parable and from the Philistines he demanded the interpretation,
the symbol was reserved, for it would not receive interpretation apart from at its (proper) time.
For the enigma of the symbols was closed and held fast
until the Son of God dawned and clarified them all.
Nor yet did Samson understand the parable that he fashioned,
140   for the time had not yet come for the mystery to be proclaimed openly.
He knew that he slew the lion and found honey,
but what the mystery of the lion and the honey was he knew not.
He made that which came to pass into a riddle for the Philistines,
that the deed could be explained just as it had occurred.

---

[31] Judg. 14:8.
[32] Judg. 14:14.
[33] Judg. 14:14. 'Bitter' in Syriac is 'strong' in Hebrew and in the LXX.

TEXT AND TRANSLATION

130
135
140
338

145	But the mystery of our Lord, who is the end of Samson's entire path,

was hidden and held fast amidst the revelations of prophecy.
Our Lord came like the day unto the denizens of darkness,
and the light of His symbol dawned and was disclosed to all the world.
The riddle which the Hebrew proposed to the Philistines
150 was not interpreted until Christ came to the world.
Death is bitter and our Lord is sweet honey,
and shining forth it came to pass that the Sweet proceeded from the bitter.
But further, death is the eater that ate all the generations of men,
yet Christ came forth from it, He who is Bread for the world to eat.[34]
155 Here it is fulfilled that the edible came forth from the eater,
but at that time who knew how to interpret these things?
Nor did Samson, who fashioned the riddle from the lion that he killed,
understand the Hidden Mystery[35] brought to pass.
Until the light, even our Lord, dawned upon creation,
160 the buried treasure of these mysteries was not revealed.
For unless the mysteries of our Lord were found in Samson,
his birth would not have been heralded by an angel.
The type of the Son was announced by the angel,
and because of Him revelations were given at diverse times.

---

[34] John 6:33–35.

[35] Hidden Mystery (*râzâ kâsyâ*): Kollamparampil lists this as a title of Christ the Saviour. See his *Salvation in Christ*, 352.

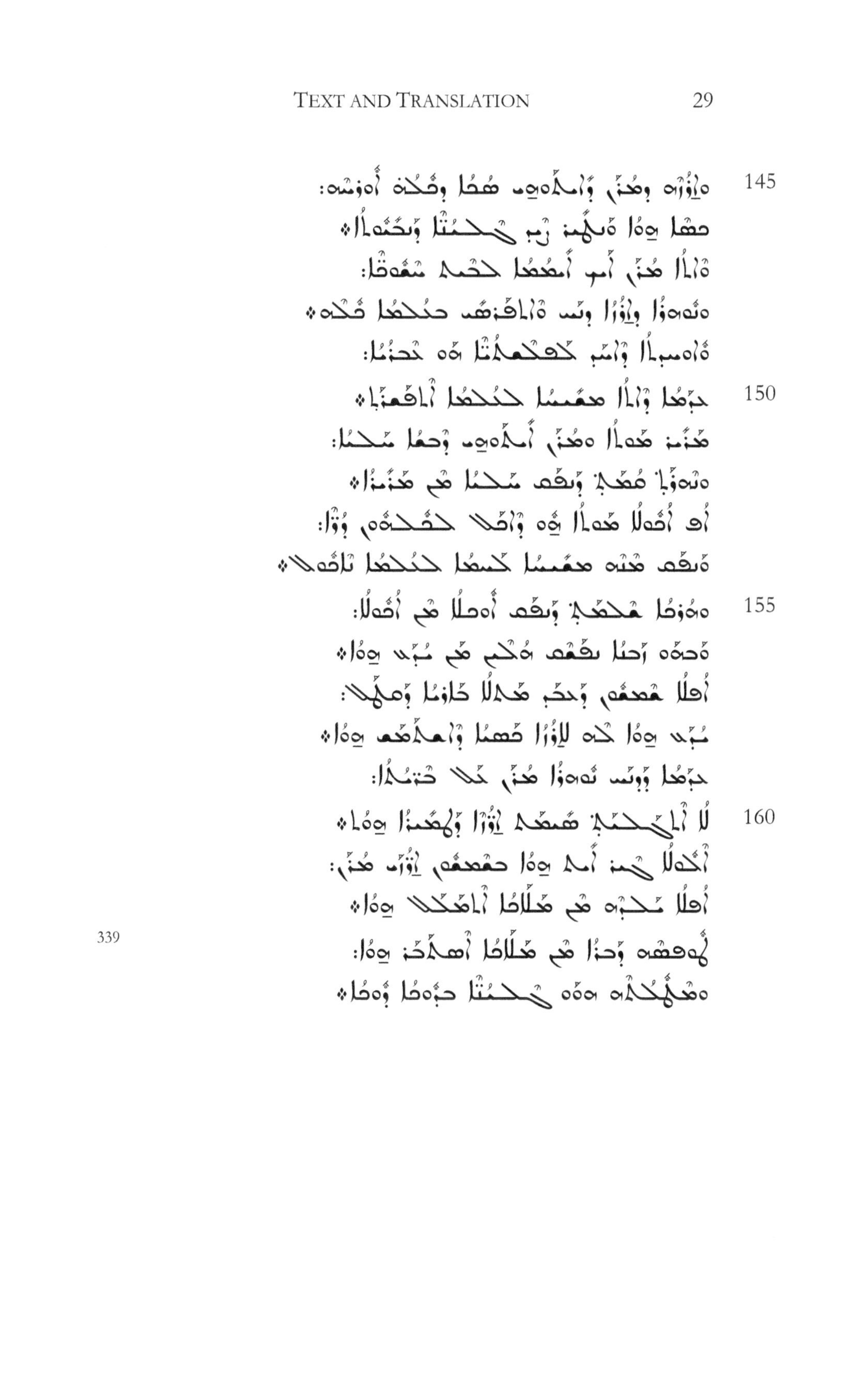

165 Everyone whose lot it has been to escort the path of the Son of God
has been honoured with revelations and the visitation of angels.
Samson is beautiful wherever he depicts the Messiah's type,[36]
and thus he composed the riddle that the sweet came forth from the bitter.[37]
Our Lord, the Word, is more delicious to the mouth than honey,[38]
170 and He is the sweet taste that sweetens the bitterness of the whole world.

SAMSON: BEAUTIFUL; ODIOUS; DEFILED

In the history of Samson there are both beautiful and blemished deeds,
but both the lofty and the lowly, all of them, deserve to be told.
Wherever he bears[39] the mystery of his Lord he is beautiful,
but wherever he falls away from prudence, he is odious and defiled.
175 He was beautiful when he slew the lion's whelp,
but odious when he was cast down by a woman's hand.
It was a comely thing for him to bring forth sweet from the bitter,
but it befit him not to reveal his secret to the woman.
Let us, then, relate all his story as it is,
180 and let it not be irksome unto us that there are both odious and beautiful deeds in it.
He made a wedding feast and took a wife, as it is written,
and he set forth the riddle of the honey and the lion to the Philistines.
Samson promised to give those changes of garments if the riddle
that he made for the Philistines was interpreted,

---

[36] The combat of Christ was foreshadowed in the fight of Samson. See Kollamparampil, *Salvation in Christ*, 339.

[37] "Our Lord is the sweet honey that proceeded from bitter death, a food which came from the eater." See Konat, *Old Testament Types of Christ*, p. 92.

[38] Ps. 118:103.

[39] The sense of the verb is 'to bear up in a procession'.

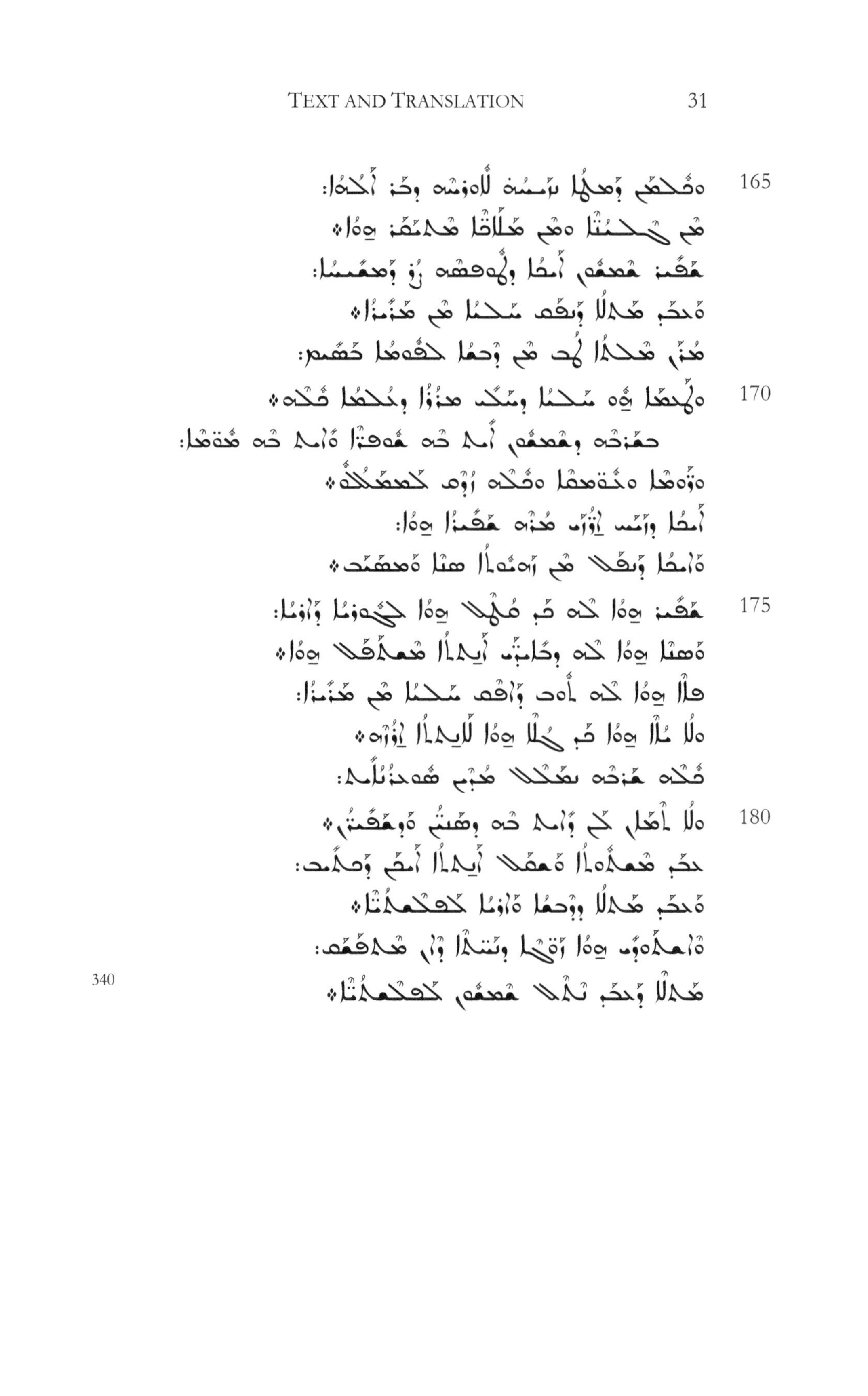

185 But straightway the woman's treachery rose up against the excellent man,
and learning his secret, made him a debtor to the Philistines.[40]
Then mighty Samson burned with indignation and in great wrath he massacred them;
being enraged, he began to contend for the slaughter of the Philistines.
He slaughtered them, plundered their corpses and took their garments,
190 so that from their own he gave to them, paying what he had promised.
He wrought mightily and his sword was drunk with their slaughter;
he disquieted them and cast consternation on their mighty men.
By reason of the riddle his bravery was revealed,
and it became known that Samson slew the lion's whelp,
195 and also that being strengthened, he wrought a slaughter and took the garments,
and the news of his mighty deed went out into all the land.
He was angry and went forth, because of the treachery that befell him,
so that for all sorts of reasons vengeance should be upon the Philistines,
thus resulting in their greater misfortune at the hands of the mighty man,
200 they gave his wife to another man, and he was greatly vexed.

SAMSON AND THE FOXES

Then Samson went and caught three hundred foxes and brought them,[41]
devising by their means to burn up all the land. He took them in pairs for the deed,
and between each pair of foxes he bound a torch and lit it.

---

[40] Judg. 14:15ff.
[41] Judg. 15:4–5.

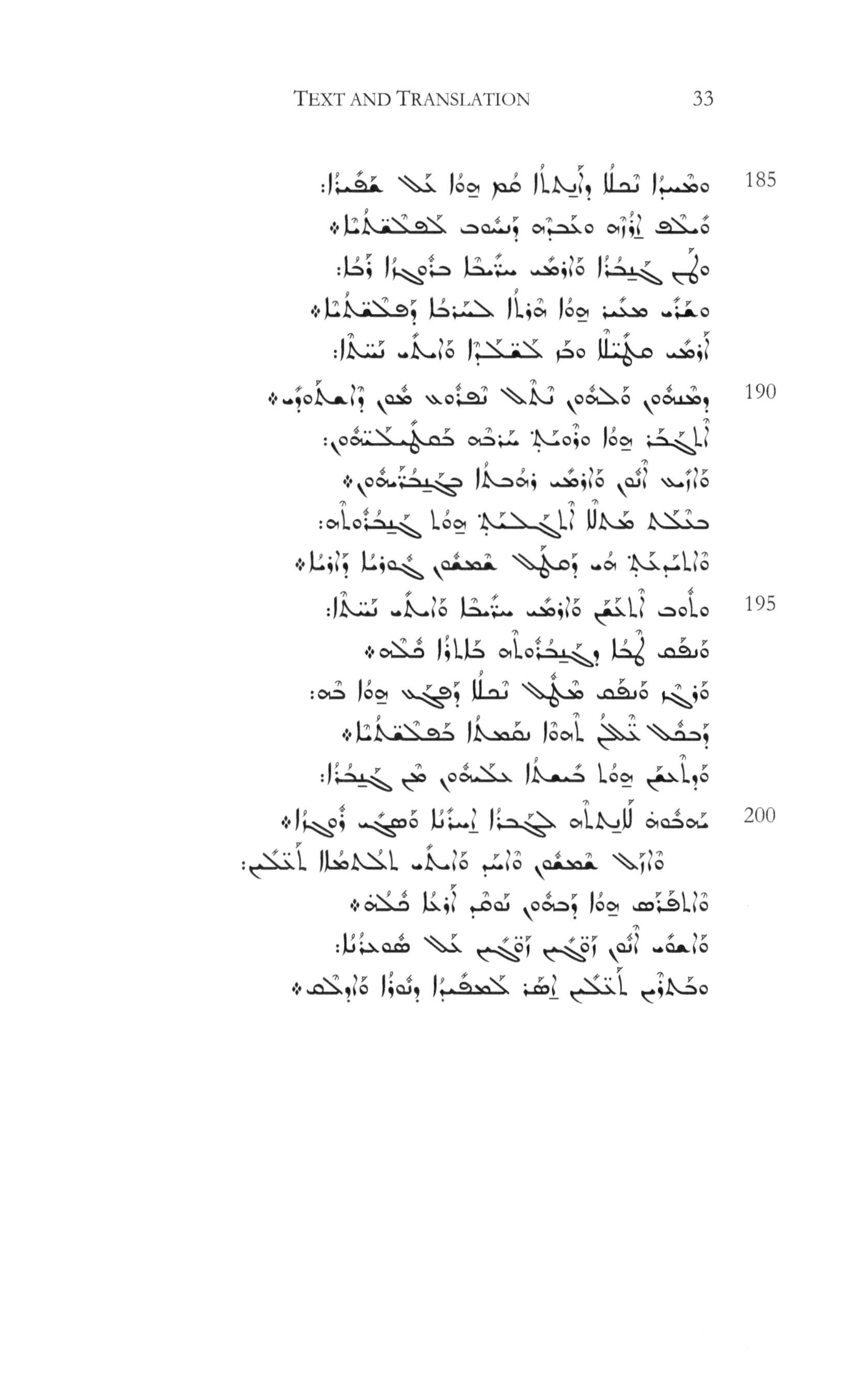

205	Then the one hundred and fifty pairs of beasts flew throughout the land,
	kindling a fire that swiftly spread out behind them.
	A novel sight then alarmed the Philistines,
	for fire was swiftly spread throughout the land by torches;
	the foxes fled so as not to be consumed by the torches,
210	but the fire ran on, being bound to the wild beasts.
	Who could catch these animals and thus stop the fire,
	or who would be able to extinguish such a conflagration?
	Throughout the whole land the fire ran and who was able
	to put out that blaze which encompassed all the region?
215	In the hay stacks[42] and in the standing wheat the fire was kindled
	and the thickets of the land that covered the face of the earth were consumed in flames.
	The conflagration overran the vineyards and the olive groves and destroyed them,
	and all their forests were destroyed by the mighty blaze.
	O the wild beasts, who can catch them so as to hold back the fire?
220	O the fire, who was there that could put it out?
	Lightning bolts of flame ran swiftly through the land;
	dreadful was the sight of the blaze as it set out upon its course.
	Who has seen, who has witnessed, who has reckoned,
	who has known how [fast] that conflagration spread?

---

[42] Judg. 15:5.

Text and Translation

341

225   What could the inhabitants of the land, who beheld the flames overrun the region,
say concerning this great fire?[43]

SAMSON SETS THE REGION ON FIRE

Then the news was spread that Samson had set fire to the whole land
and, moreover, the wonder was added to its fellows.[44]
At this deed the Philistines sounded the alarm,
230   striving to capture Samson and make a mockery of him who had burned their land.
Thus the Philistines went up in an assault against the Hebrews,[45]
but Samson's compatriots seized him because they feared.
They bound him firmly with new ropes[46]
And they handed him over to the Philistines that they might mock him.
235   Then the power of God shone upon the Nazirite
And he mightily broke and cast off those bonds.
He found there, as it is written, a jawbone of an ass,[47]
and instead of a weapon, which he could not find, he took up this bone.
A naked man, he fell upon the ranks of the Philistines
240   and massacred them, heaping up piles and piles of their corpses.
He slew a thousand men with that jawbone singlehanded,
for the Spirit of the Lord had taken hold of him in that conflict.
Weaponry was confounded because Samson did not seek a weapon,
and the sword was powerless, for the bone took the victory.

---

[43] By his description Mar Jacob seems to indicate that the foxes typify the apostles who went forth in pairs to burn up idolatry and unbelief. He does not, however, say this explicitly.

[44] I.e., Samson's other marvelous works.

[45] Judg. 15:9,10.

[46] Judg. 15:11,12.

[47] Judg. 15:15.

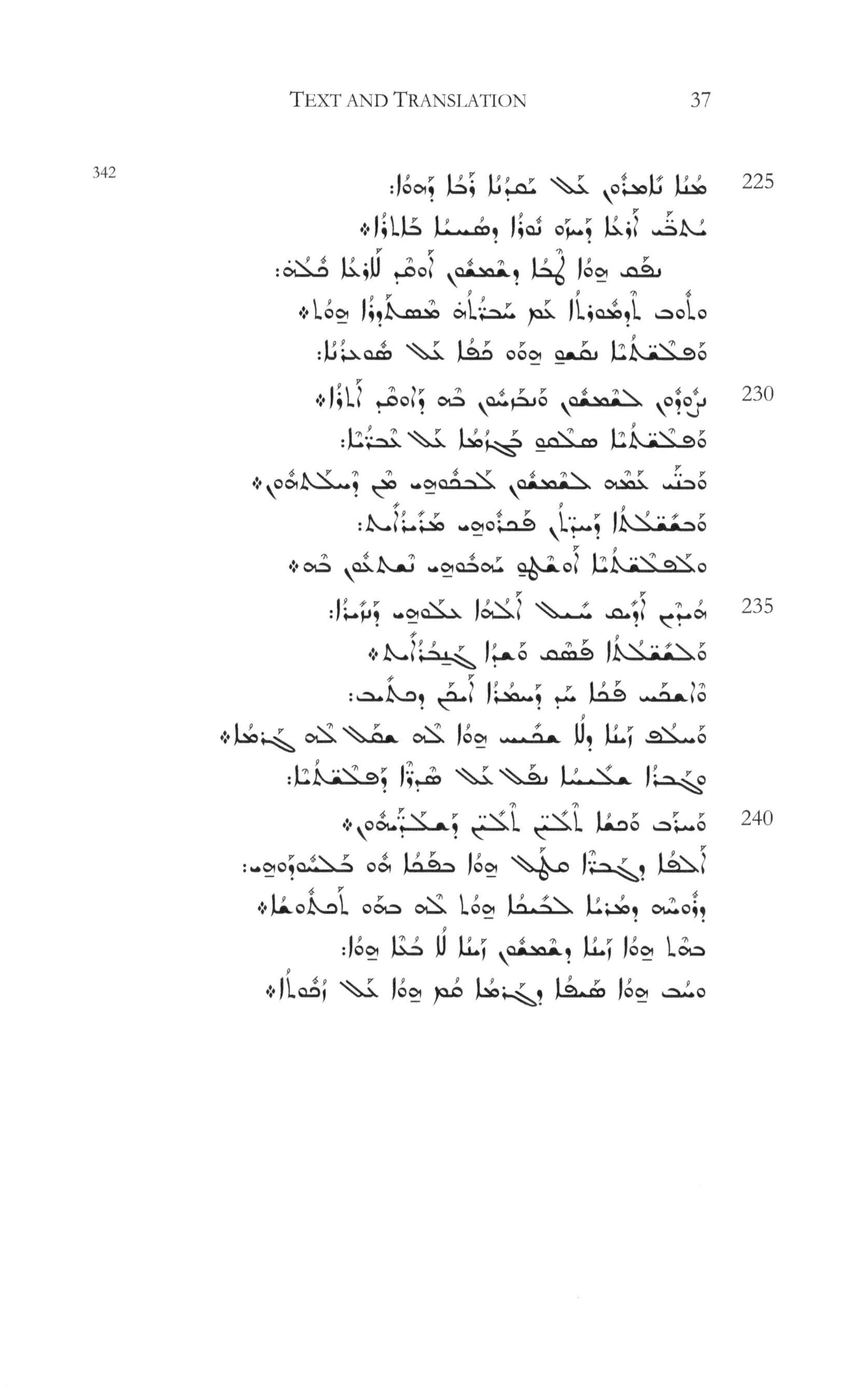

342

245   The bows and bowstrings and the arrows of the Philistines were powerless,
for by a single jawbone the brave man laid waste to an entire legion.
The forgers of weapons were put to shame by this battle,
for here the forged weapon in no wise helped its master.
Bucklers and shields were of no help to the warriors,
250   for Samson took up only a bone and slaughtered a thousand men.
It made a mockery of all the weapons of those warriors,
for in the contest one dry bone took the victory.
Samson cast down the thousand as though they had been a lone man,
and he taught[48] the whole land that it is the Lord who has power over victory.

SAMSON THIRSTS AND THE LORD PROVIDES

255   But growing thirsty while he fought, Samson desired water;
and the Lord opened a hollow place in the bone so that he could drink.[49]
From one wonder yet another wonder sprang,[50]
so that by the twain Samson's Lord might be glorified.
By a dry bone he slew a thousand men as he fought,
260   and when he thirsted for water, water gushed forth for him from the bone.
[The Lord] bored through that arid bone and gave him water,
so that the sign that He wrought would be great and awesome.
It was a miracle that without a weapon Samson triumphed,
and again it was a miracle that water was found within the bone.

---

[48] A play on the word 'thousand' in Syriac.

[49] Judg. 15:19.

[50] Wonder (*tehrâ*) is the beginning of ecstasy. The roots of wonder lie deep in Syriac tradition. Already Theodore of Mopsuestia says that *tehrâ* about God is the "unique science." Ephrem is constantly amazed in wonder at the Incarnation and at the Eucharist, but also at all the created world as both Scripture and the natural world are revelatory. Ephrem sees *tehrâ* as a revelation of the New World. See M.T. Hansbury, "'Insight without sight': wonder as an aspect of revelation in the Discourses of Isaac the Syrian", *Journal of the Canadian Society for Syriac Studies* 8 (2008), 60–73.

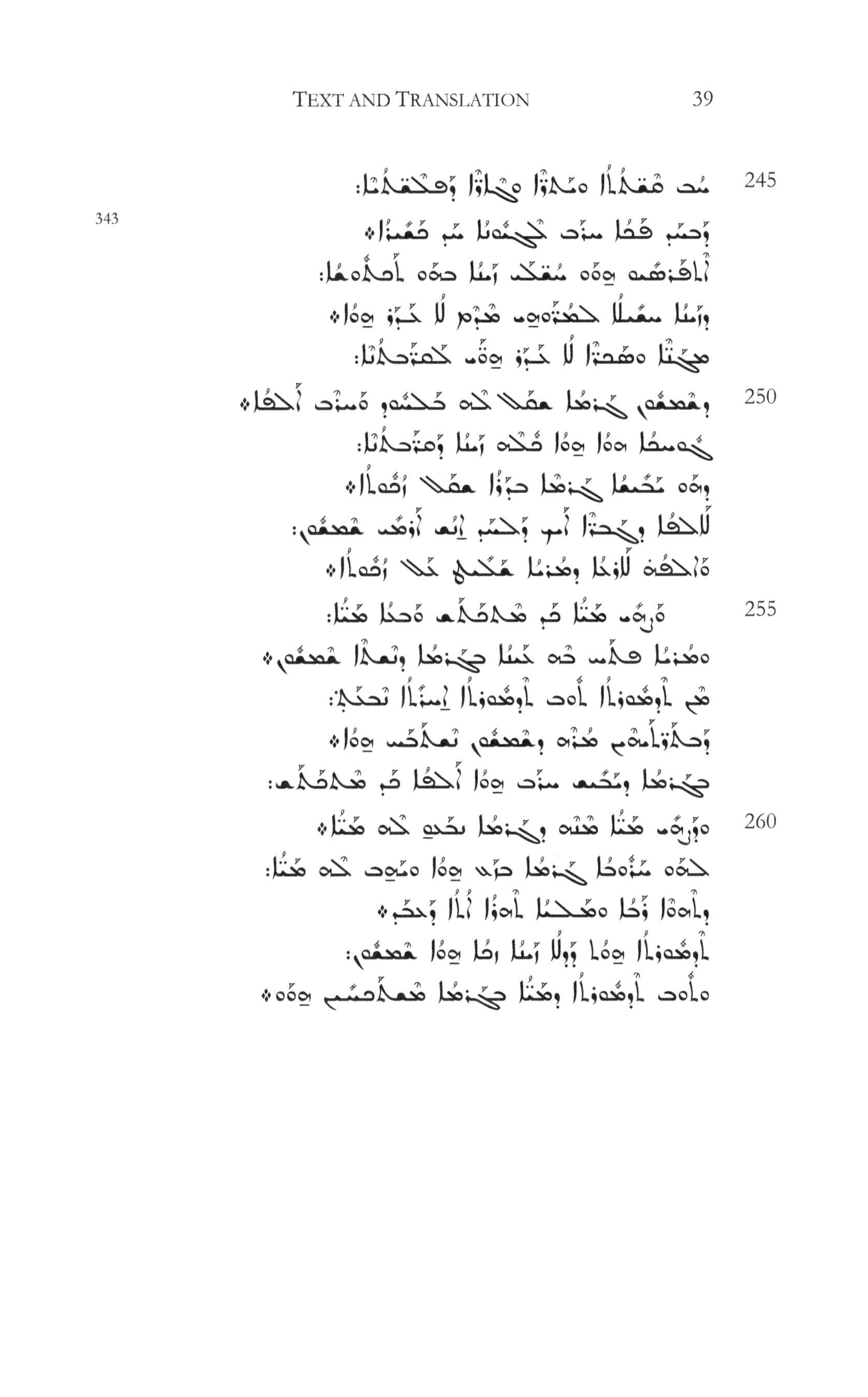

343

265 A spring gushed forth from that bone in Samson's presence,
and I should be amazed if the wonder was accomplished just that he might drink.
The wonder was a great one, like that done by the hands of Moses,[51]
for there the rock and here the bone became a spring.
The region was astonished at the marvelous works that were done
270 by the hands of Samson, the mighty champion of God's household.

Samson and the harlot

Now after Samson wrought this great miracle,
he entered a city and found a harlot, as it is written.[52]
But what shall I say concerning Samson, I know not,
for his history troubles and perplexes me.
275 I hear that he prayed and that water sprang forth and he drank,
but shortly thereafter I find him with a harlot.
He went forth and massacred a thousand as a single man,
but then he betrayed himself, a woman sheared his hair and he became a mockery.
For what cause did the Nazirite of the Lord go to the harlot?
280 His tale confuses me and I know not what to say of it.
The Lord is very condescending and forbearing towards mankind,
and wherever men fall it is not He that seeks to cast them down.
The mighty deeds that Samson wrought were God's,
whereas the others which were uncomely were his own.

---

[51] Ex. 17:6.
[52] Judg. 16:1.

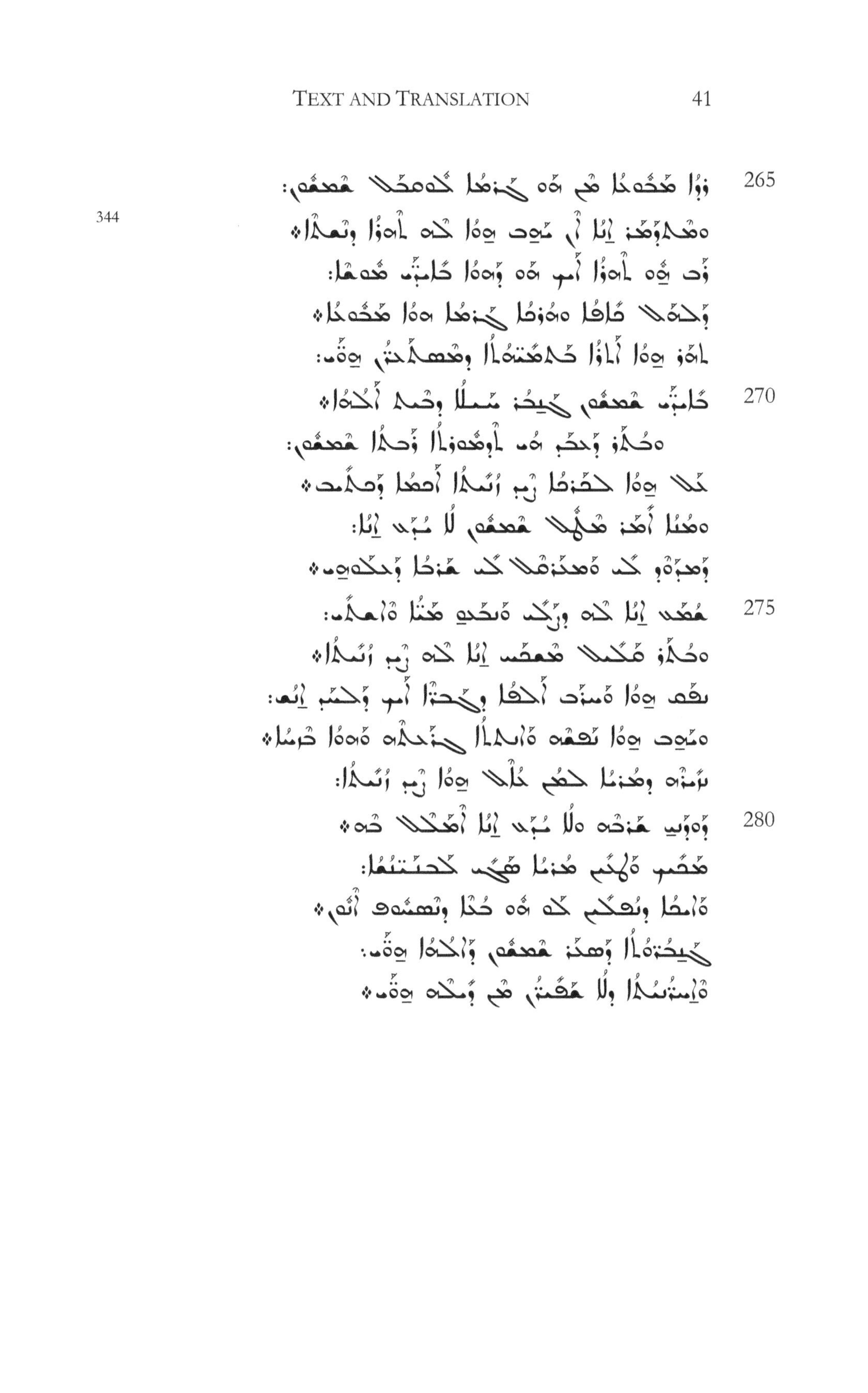

344

285 God did not tell him to go to the harlot;
he himself wished to go in, and the Lord did not compel him, since he was free.
He thirsted and when he asked, the Lord gave him water and he drank,
but when he wished to go to the harlot, he went in as he willed.
How the Lord will judge the Last Judgment
290 is not your affair; trouble not yourself about things that do not concern you.
But possibly this also, [I mean] that Samson went down to the harlot,
[it] was permitted him by providence, that he might fall for your sake,
so that he might be for you a mirror that reveals your blemishes,
And you might see yourself and not fall as he fell.

SHEOL: THE LORD; SAMSON

295 He went, then, into the town to be with the harlot,
but the inhabitants of the place were aroused and they gathered together to capture him.
Samson arose at midnight for his deed,
he roused himself mightily for the miracle.
He went up to the closed gates [of the city] and wrenched them
300 and he lifted them up upon his shoulders as he departed.[53]
Raising up the lintels, the bars and the gates, he carried them and departed;
thus did the mighty man despise and shame his guards.
This was a miracle that none could do save Samson,
for he carried away the doorposts, the gates and the bars upon his shoulders.

---

[53] Judg. 16:3.

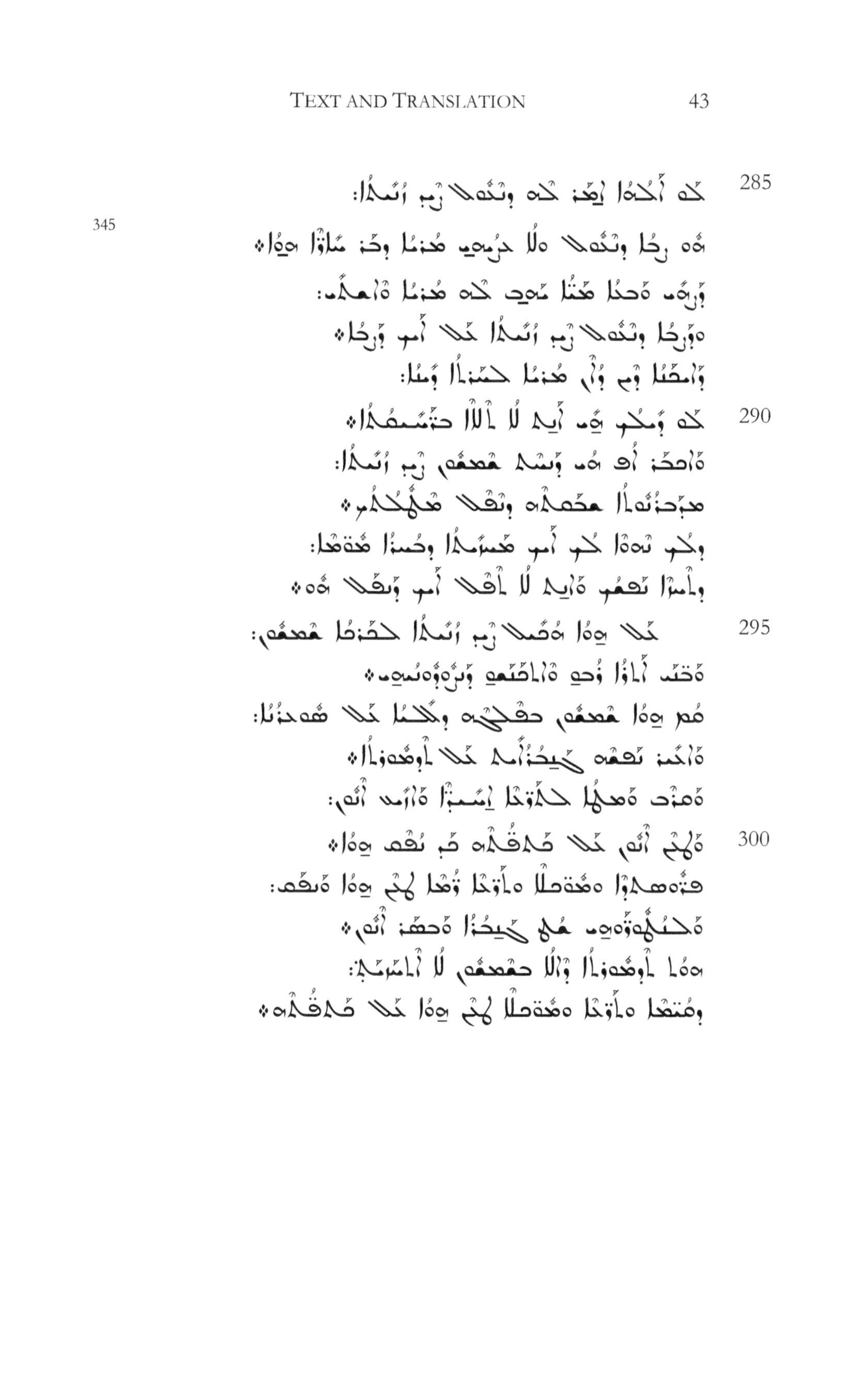

305 He wished not to open the gates and depart like a fugitive,
but he lifted them up and removed them like a champion.
The fastened gates did not stand before him when he departed,
for the mystery of the Son guided this Hebrew man.
Sheol[54] is a harlot, and all generations were her men;
310 She seized our Lord to bring Him to herself like the rest.
So He went, falling asleep, and the door of the tomb was closed upon Him,
And men stood crazily guarding Him, as it was with Samson.
But the Saviour arose from the grave and broke down
all the bulwarks of Sheol as He departed, and they stood not before Him.
315 This mystery brought Samson to the harlot,
for she too is a Sheol, because she destroys whoever goes to her.
The type that was portrayed by Samson gave him the strength
To lift up the gates and the iron bars and to depart as he did.
Many men had gone to this harlot of the Philistines,
320 But no one save Samson broke down the gates of the town.
All generations entered into Sheol, the ravager of men,
and save our Lord none threw down its bulwarks and quickened its dead.
Such was the mystery that was kindled within this Hebrew,
and he pulled up the gates of the fortress when he left from the harlot.

---

[54] Sheol is the symbol of all evils, bondages and captivity, once prefigured in the history of the chosen people, that indicate the deeper spiritual bondages and captivity of Adam/humanity. "The shattering of Sheol is prefigured by Samson in the history which became actualized in the Resurrection of the Lord," see T. Kollamparampil, *Salvation in Christ according to Jacob of Serugh* (Bangalore, 2001), 174.

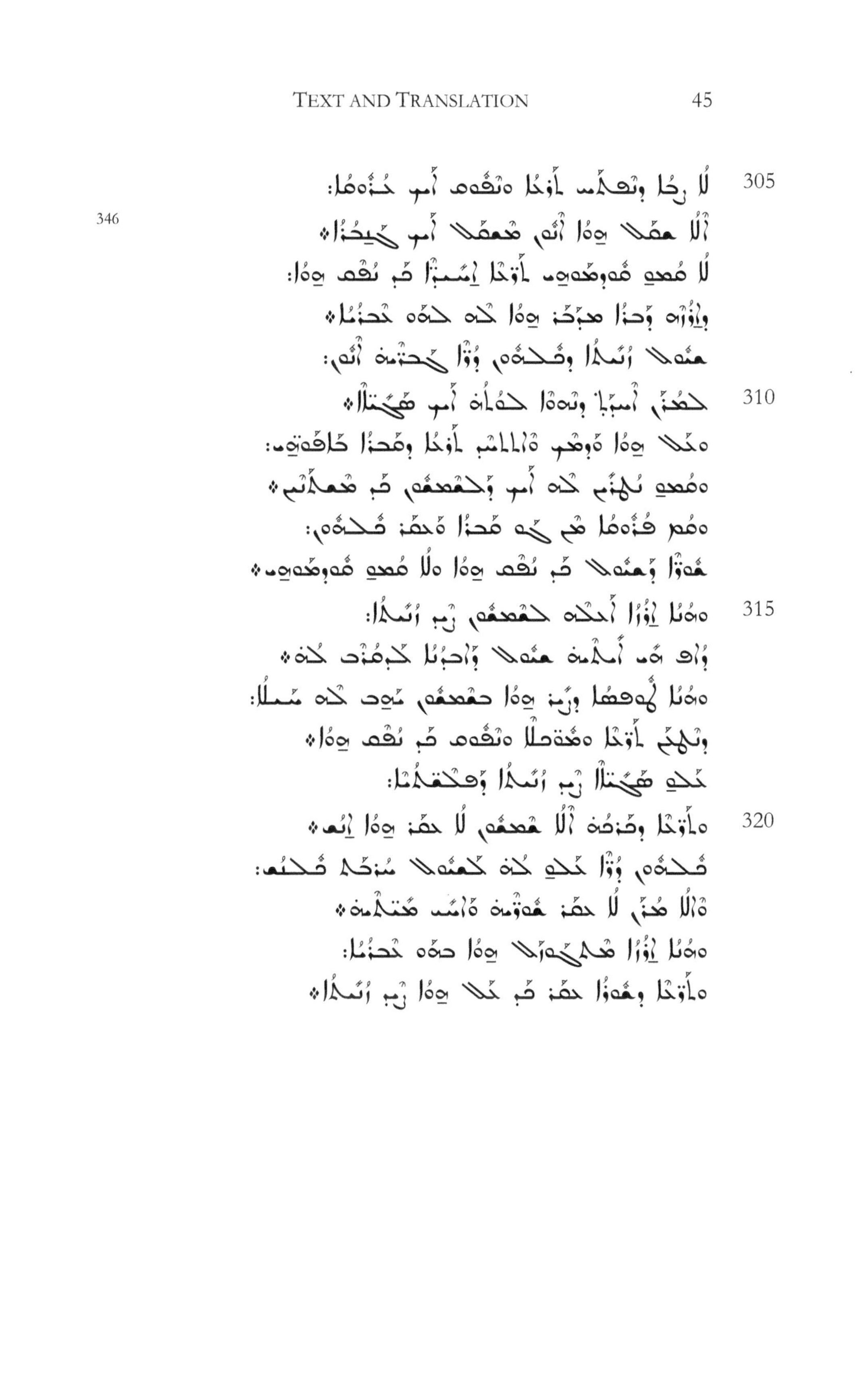

346

325 He confounded the Philistines by his might,
and depicted an image of those who guarded the tomb of the Son.

SAMSON ENABLED BY THE MYSTERIES OF HIS LORD

By the mysteries of his Lord he was strengthened for a mighty deed,
even Samson the Nazirite, who shone forth in the land of the Philistines.
He, that heroic man, set the gates and bars upon his shoulders,
330 climbed up and placed them upon the mount of Hebron, as it is written.[55]
Now after these things the mysteries abandoned him to trial, [to determine]
whether he would triumph by himself without [divine] aid.
Once again he loved a woman, a harlot, and went to her,
but from the beginning she joined the plot for his ruin.
335 She devised a scheme, she laid snares, and she hid her net,
so that the young stag would become entangled and be put to scorn.
She began cajoling and wheedling him in her slyness
to reveal to her the cause of his great strength.[56]
She spoke to him with treachery and artfulness,
340 with the intimacy that women employ towards their men.
At times she asked to show her [the cause of] his great strength,
and at times she remained silent, lest she make him aware of her treachery.
But at other times she humoured him, then pressed and persuaded him
to reveal to her the mysteries of his heart,[57] that she might mock him.

---

[55] Judg. 16:3.
[56] Judg. 16:5ff.
[57] Another reading is 'of his Lord'.

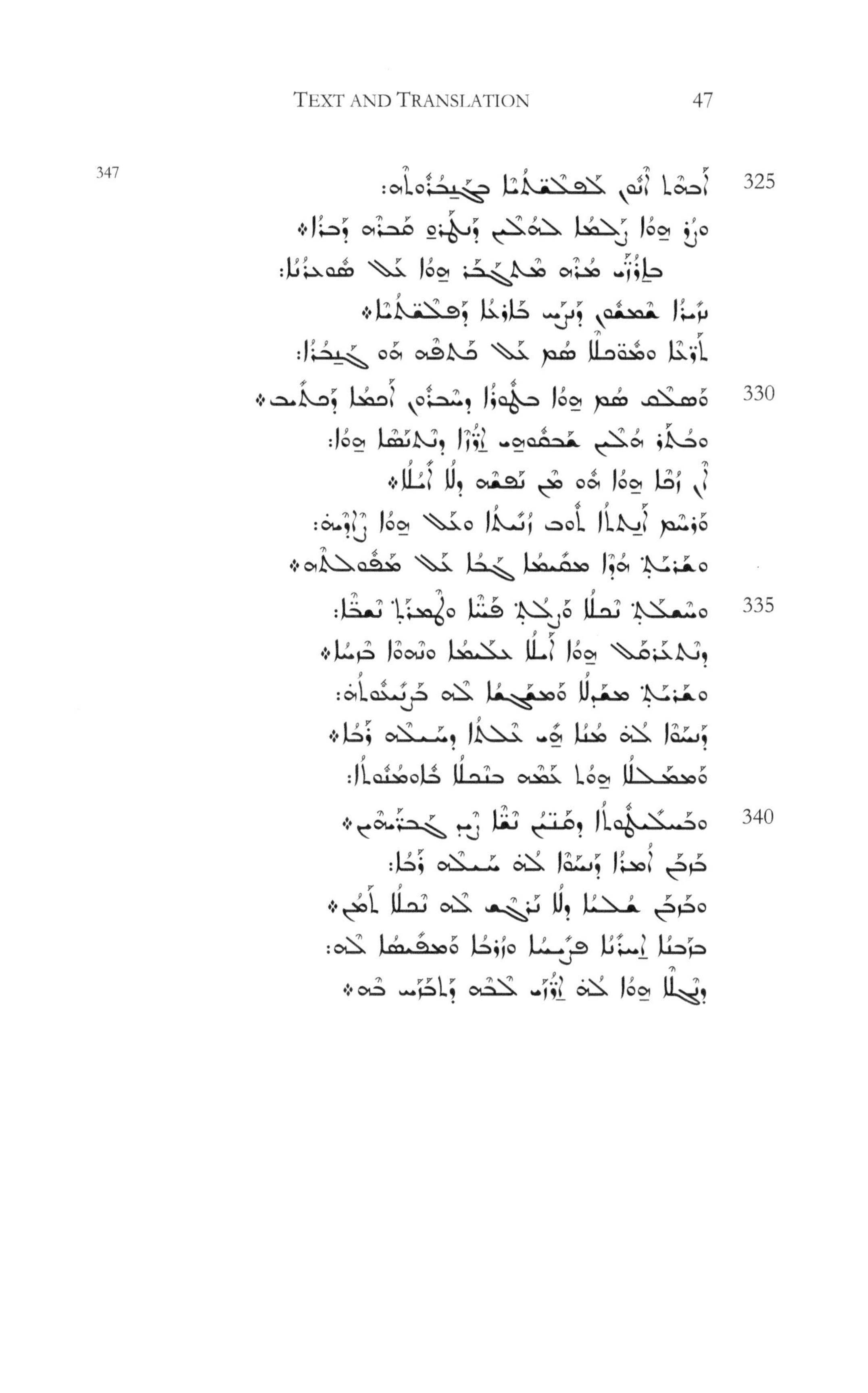

347

345	For a short time he withstood the harlot,
	and said to her one thing in place of another:
	"If by seven fresh bowstrings I am bound,
	I shall become weak,"[58] and the woman did just what he told her.
	But when she woke him to see whether in truth he had lost his strength,
350	as though they were smoke, the bowstrings that bound him could not withstand him.
	And like as when a mighty blaze breathes upon
	fine threads of wool and flax, so he broke them.

SAMSON AND DELILAH

	The harlot, however, was persistent in the matter
	and became not despondent because her first snare did not catch him.
355	Again she cajoled him and again he said to the polluted woman,
	"If I am bound with ropes, I shall become weak."[59]
	Thus she did, and with tightly woven ropes
	she bound him while he slept, but when she roused him, he broke them.
	The great strength of his being a Nazirite seethed within him,
360	and thereby he defeated and triumphed over all forces.
	He broke the bonds as though fire had consumed them,
	and neither ropes nor bowstrings could withstand him.
	Yet once more the harlot craftily and persistently
	strove to lay a snare that might not slip, but would catch him.

---

[58] Judg. 16:7.
[59] Judg. 16:11.

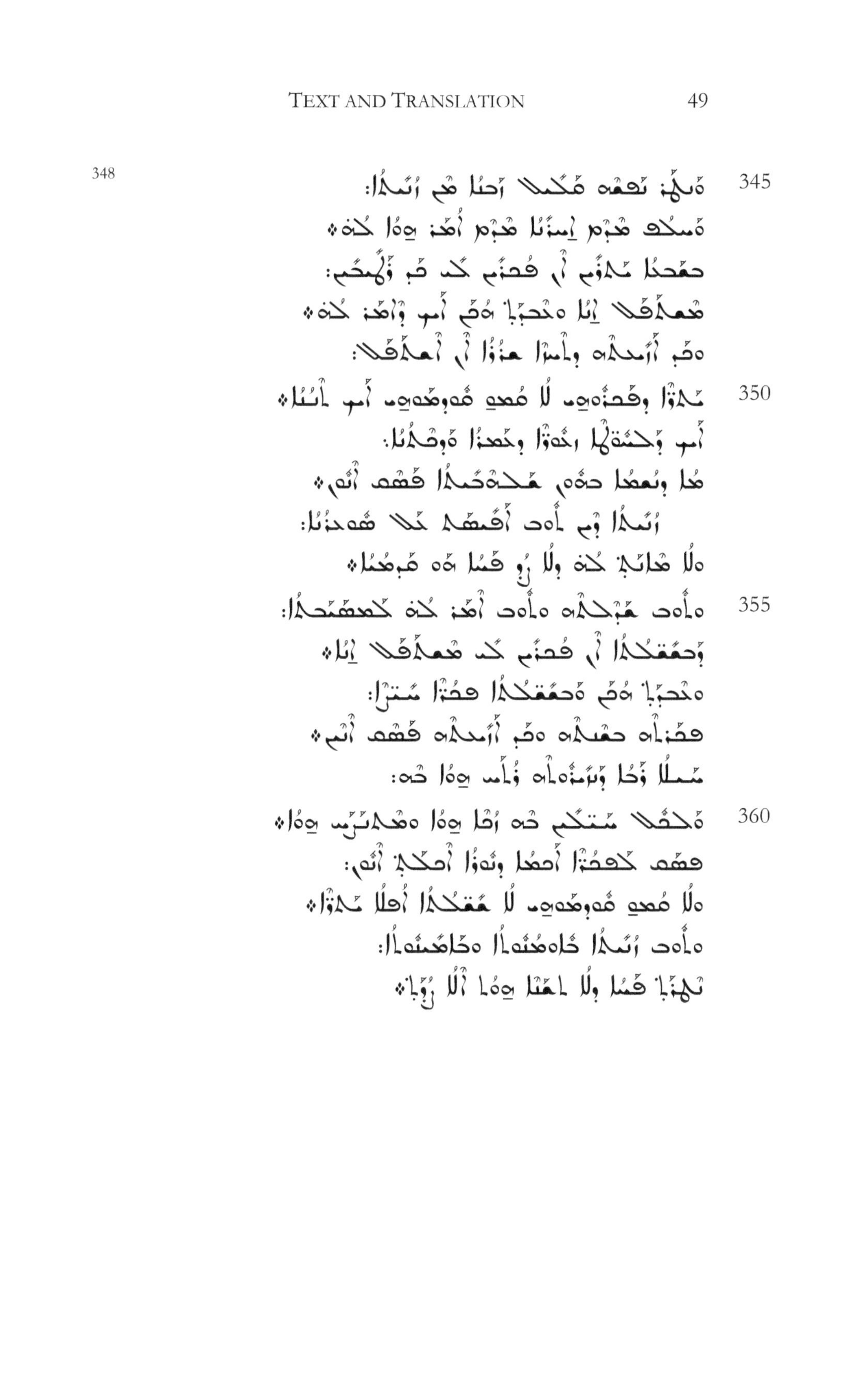

348

365 And she coaxed him and again he told her something else,
because her enticements were pressing and continual.
"If the hair of my head," he said, "is woven like a web
with the pin, straightway my strength will vanish and I shall become weak."[60]
And she, who was diligent in laying snares and wearied not,
370 wove his hair carefully, even as he told her.
But when she woke him, he lifted up the pins with his hair
and moved the Philistines to great wonder.
But that beguiler and layer of snares for murder
desponded not; again she strove assiduously to commit the deed.
375 Once more she cajoled him, persuaded him, wearied him;
she lamented, she jested, she urged, she quarreled and she afflicted him.
By all devices, by all enticements and by all pretenses
she troubled Samson; then he revealed his secret and became a weakling.
He showed her what the cause of his strength was
380 and from whence there was found in him indomitable power.
"A Nazirite am I from my mother's womb," he said to her,
"and a razor has never come upon my head, even from my birth.
But if I be shaven and the hair upon my head be taken away,
The power of my being a Nazirite will swiftly depart and I shall be weak."[61]

---

[60] Judg. 16:13.
[61] Judg. 16:17.

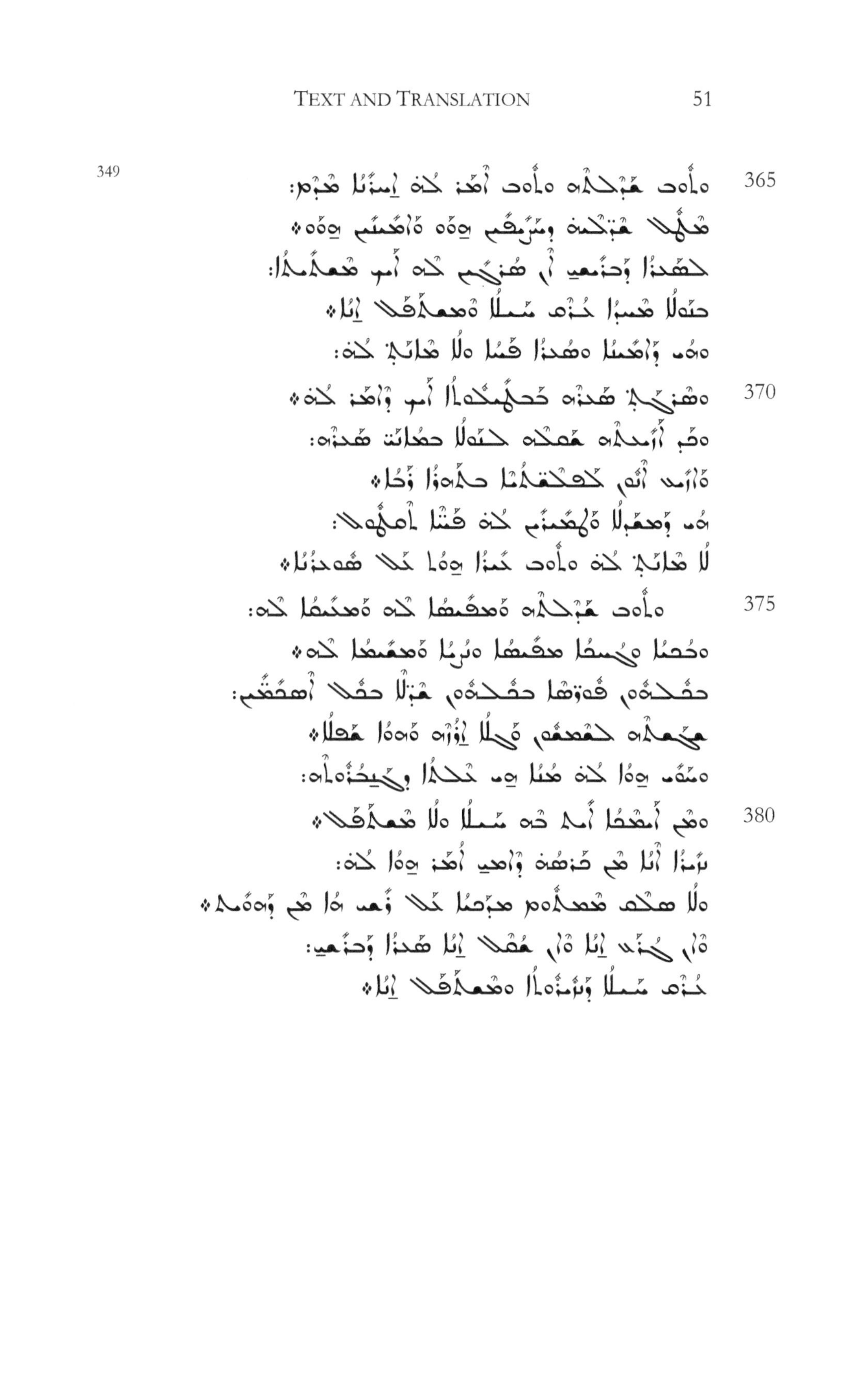

349

385	As soon as that most treacherous woman captured the secret from him,
	she sent for and called the Philistines for the deed.
	She caused him to fall asleep, she shaved him and she delivered him up,
	and when she woke him, he stood up as feeble as a weakling.
	The mighty man fell into the woman's hands and she spared him not;
390	she cut off and hurled down the lofty and beautiful cedar.
	She dug a pit, thrust down the lion, and he fell, being weak;
	the strong man became a mockery of the woman who vanquished him.
	The entire land learned of women's treachery against Samson,
	and the proverb was created, "Keep the words of thy mouth from thy wife."[62]
395	The second Eve cast down the second Adam, that is Samson,
	and he fell from the lofty height where he stood.
	She stole from him all the power of his being a Nazirite,
	and he became a weakling and a great mockery for the Philistines.
	Eve expelled Adam from Paradise;
400	Delilah took from Samson his rank of being a Nazirite.
	At the world's beginning Adam set up a mirror[63] for you,
	and in the middle point Samson placed another, if you will but look.
	Behold, Delilah and Eve can be seen clearly
	by the man who desires to preserve himself from ruin.

---

[62] Cf., line 406.

[63] Samson through his successes and failures has become a mirror of the free will in Adam/humanity. Whenever he stood in conformity with the will of God or in the Spirit of prophecy, he succeeded and at other times he fell down like Adam. The mirror (*mahzîtâ*) is used as a metaphor in spiritual teaching. It may be identified as anything that can reflect divine reality. In Syriac literature mirror imagery is found throughout St. Ephrem particularly in his Letter to Publius. See S.P. Brock, "The imagery of the spiritual mirror in Syriac tradition", *Journal of the Canadian Society for Syriac Studies* 5 (2005), 3–17. See also Ephrem, *Hymns on Faith*, 67,8: *The Scriptures are laid out like a mirror / and the person whose eye is luminous / sees therein the image of Divine Reality.*

TEXT AND TRANSLATION   53

405   By these two a woman's treachery is expounded to you,
and therefore the prophet cries out, "Keep the words of your mouth from your thy wife."
Alas, the mighty man, Samson the Nazirite, has become a mockery,
a great laughingstock and an infamous name for generations to come.
The strong man who vanquished in battle the lion's whelp
410   was by a woman's hand brought low, an overwhelming disgrace.
Like a viper she bit the Nazirite and his hair fell away,
and he became feeble, wretched, weak and tottering.

SAMSON TO BE A MIRROR

Then the Philistines gathered to view the lion,
to make sport of the man who had killed so many of their number.
415   Raving, they blinded his eyes and destroyed his beauty;[64]
they extinguished the spark of light whereby he could see.
They made a hideous blemish upon that great beauty,
the mighty man fell under great humiliation.
They brought and bound him and he ground at the mill of the prison;[65]
420   there he was found, a source of great festivity for the Philistines.
The words which are found in the divine Scriptures
were placed there by the Creator because of the benefit that lies within them.
Let him who wishes to gain life read and be enriched
by the treasures that are buried in the passages of Scripture![66]

---

[64] Judg. 16:21.
[65] Judg. 16:21.
[66] Cf. John 5:31.

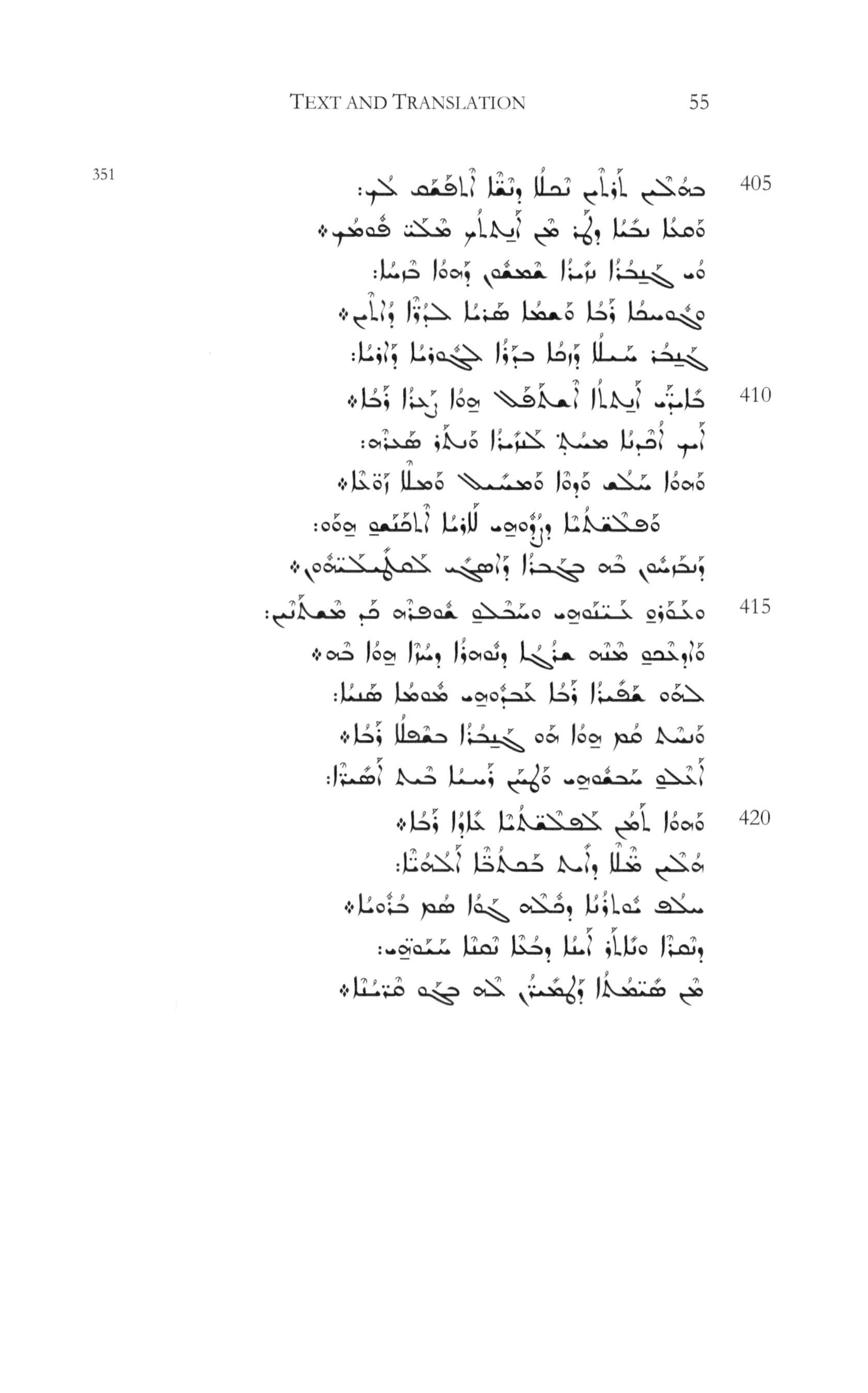

351

425 Samson grinds; who then shall not flee from the harlot
and keep his path clear, lest her smoke reach him?
She made the Nazirite a shaven man because he consented to her;
Who does not tremble, hearing of the deeds[67] of vice?
She yoked to the millstone the mighty man who slew the lion;
430 who then would hearken to her, save a fool who, like her, is wicked?
Let Samson be a mirror for men who are sagacious,
and let them hate the deeds, the enticements and the treacheries of vice!
Samson fell into the hands of those whose slain
and whose corpses were daily piled up in their region.
435 Out of joy they made a great festival to the idols,[68]
as though Dagon[69] had bound Samson who had so vexed them.
Both men and women of the Philistines assembled
for that great feast which they made on account of Samson.
When because of wine they were besides themselves from their merry-making,
440 they said, "Let that Hebrew be brought to dance and amuse us![70]
Let Samson be brought, let all the people witness his mockery,
And let every man rejoice who sees his humiliation, and let him taunt him"!

SAMSON SHAVEN, BLINDED AND MADE A LAUGHING STOCK UNTO THE PHILISTINES

Then came great Samson, fallen from his greatness,
the lofty man who came down from the lofty rank where he stood,

---

[67] Lit., 'words'.

[68] Judg. 16:23.

[69] Dagon: an ancient deity. The Hebrew Bible mentions him as the national god of the Philistines with temples at Ashdod (1 Sam. 5:2–7) and in Gaza (Judges 16:2–3).

[70] Judg. 16:25.

425	:
	:
	:
430	
	:
	:
435	:
	:
	:
440	
	:
	:

445   the chosen one who went astray, who desired, and became the intimate of a harlot,
the Nazirite from whom the beauty of his Naziritehood was taken away.
He was shaven, blinded and made a laughingstock for the Philistines,
and they ridiculed him by forcing him to dance and entertain them.
The wretched man, however, from his great affliction and grief
450   was moved to take vengeance upon the Philistines.
He persuaded them to bring him near the pillars of the house
as one who was weary and needed to rest from exhaustion.
Then he drew nigh and grasped the two pillars of the great house
and cried to the Lord to strengthen him in his weakness.
455   Here he teaches us that even when a man has fallen away from God,
yet if he cries out to the Lord with pain of heart, He will hearken to him.
For the Lord never withholds His mercy from those who entreat Him,
not even when a man should fall into unseemly lusts.
As soon as contrition enters the soul
460   and drives it from the filth of the lusts whereby it was befouled,
it is moved to prayer to God with special fervour
and He hearkens to the soul, though it be covered with ten thousand blemishes.
Samson prayed to God after destroying his rank of a Nazirite,
after the power of God had withdrawn and forsaken him,

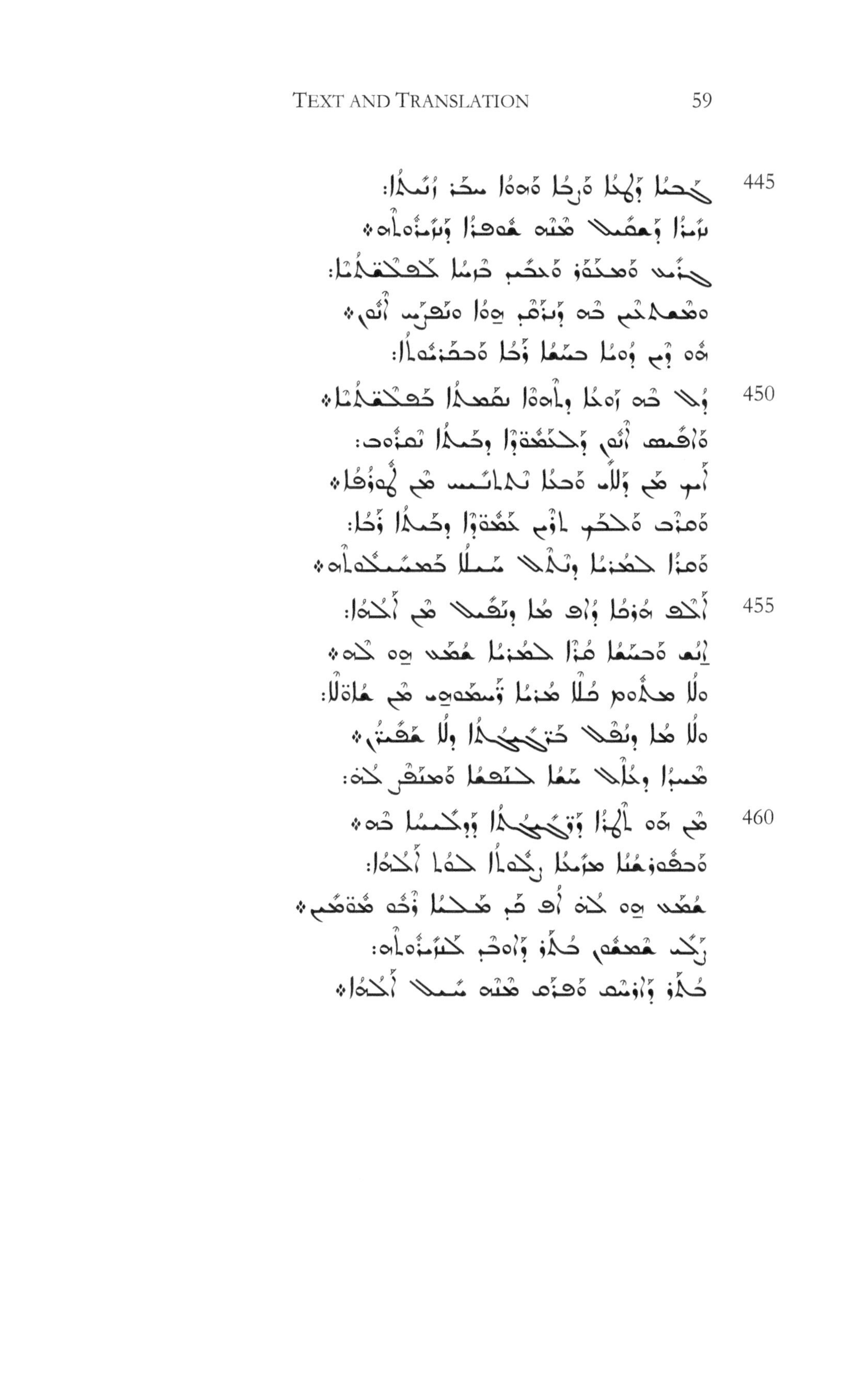

465 after he lost his senses with the harlot,
after he voluntarily handed himself over to derision,
after the Lord surrendered and gave him over to the Philistines
and did not become his protector when he was blinded at their hands.

GOD HEARD SAMSON'S PRAYER OF CONTRITION AND GRANTED HIS REQUEST

After, therefore, all these things that had come to pass, Samson prayed,
470 and because he prayed with contrition, the Lord heard him and granted him his request.
He beheld within himself that he had ruined the beauty of being a Nazirite
and that the power of his manliness had been stripped from him,
that the Lord's Spirit which flourished in him had fled,
And that being assailed he could not of himself triumph in the fight.
475 Contrition entered and shook his soul because of these things
and the man was moved to make supplication with a broken heart.
The Lord, who seeks to heal[71] those who are broken of heart[72]
hearkened to Samson and stretching out His hand, He gave him strength.
Then with power he assailed the pillars of the house and it fell,
480 and he turned the pagans' festival into lamentation by his deed.
He toppled the pillars and the house of the Philistines collapsed;
in his anger he brought destruction upon those seated above and below.
Thus he filled the place with the stacks of their corpses,
and the land stank from the heaps of dead bodies that lay there in piles.

---

[71] Lit., 'to bind up'.
[72] Cf., Ps. 146:3.

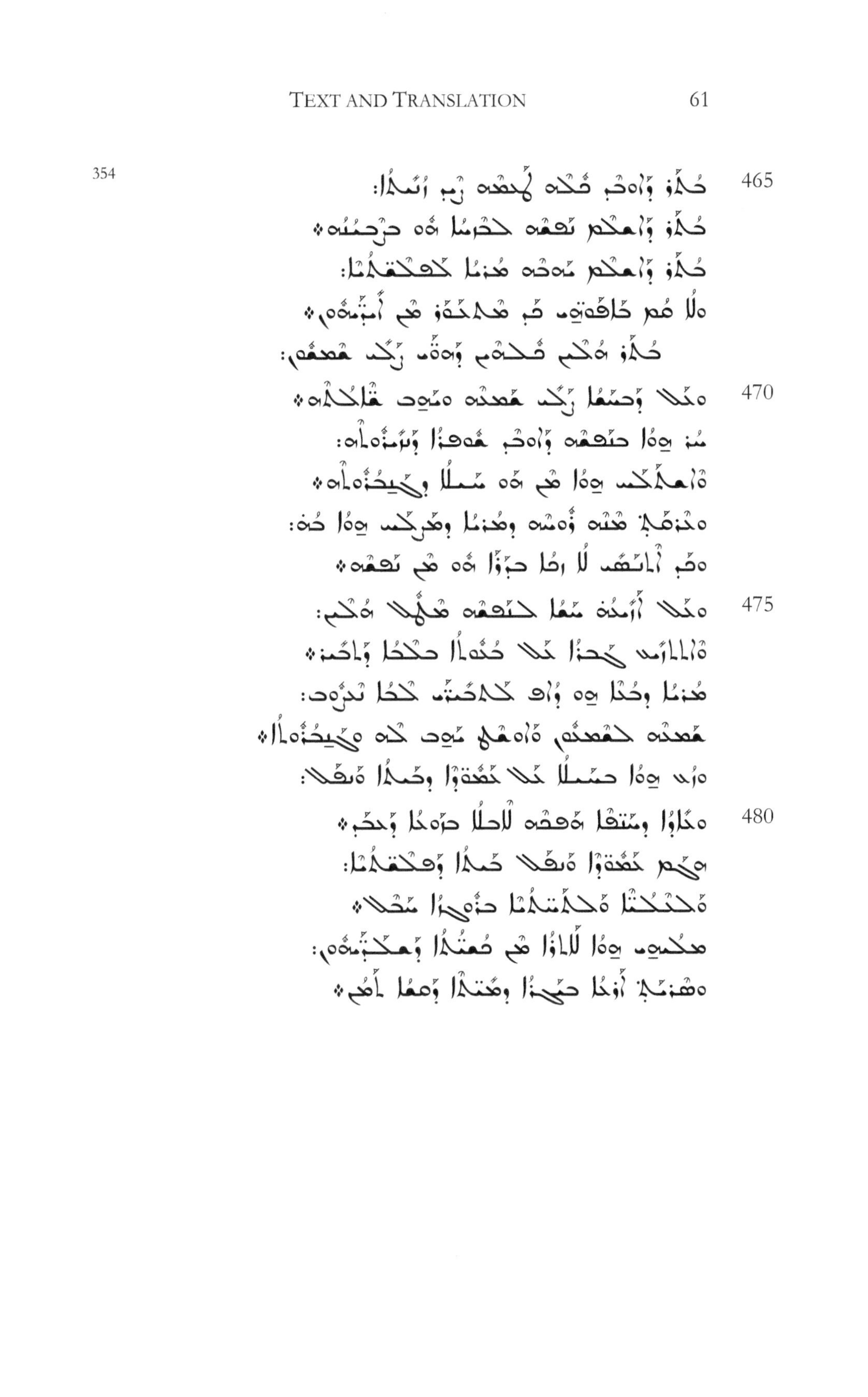

354

485   This last slaughter wrought by the hands of Samson surpassed all the former.[73]

Blessed be He who hearkens to the one who cries out to Him! [Amen]

The End of the Homily on Samson

---

[73] Cf., Judges 16:30.

485 ܡܫܘܚܬܐ ܐܚܪܬܐ ܕܩܝܪܝܠܘܣ ܚܕܬܐ ܐܢܝ:
ܕܐܝܬ ܦܘܩܕܢ ܕܐܒܘ ܗܘ ܘܚܢܐ ܕܒܪܐ ܕܝܠܗ܀

ܥܠܡ ܥܐܡܕܐ ܕܟܠ ܦܘܩܕܢ.

BIBLIOGRAPHY OF WORKS CITED

M. Albert (tr.), *Les Lettres de Jacques de Saroug*, Patrimoine Syriaque 3 (Kaslik, 2004).

H. Alfeyev, *The Spiritual World of Isaac the Syrian* (Kalamazoo MI, 2000).

A. Becker, "Polishing the Mirror, Some Thoughts on Syriac Sources and Early Judaism", in *Envisioning Judaism Studies in Honor of Peter Schäfer* (Tubingen: Mohr Siebeck, 2013) Volume 2.

S. Beggiani, *Early Syriac Theology* (Washington, D.C. : Catholic University of America Press, 2014).

——, "The Typological Approach of Syriac Sacramental Theology," *TS* 64 (2003): 543–57.

B. M. Boulos Sony, "La Methode Exégètique de Jacques de Saroug," *PdO* 9 ('79–'80): 67–103.

T. Bou Mansour, *La Théologie de Jacques de Saroug* Vol I (Lebanon, 1993).

S. Brock, "The Imagery of the Spiritual Mirror in Syriac Literature," *JCSSS* 5 (2005): 3–17.

——, *Jacob of Serug's Homily on the Veil on Moses' Face*, (tr.) TeCLA 20 (Gorgias Press, 2009).

——, "Jewish Traditions in Syriac Sources," *JJS* 30 (1979), 212–32.

——, *The Luminous Eye*, Cistercian Publications (Kalamazoo MI, 1992).

R. Chesnut, *Three Monophysite Christologies: Severus of Antioch, Philoxenus of Mabbug and Jacob of Serug* (Oxford, 1976).

A. Elkhoury, "Jesus Christ, the Eye of Prophecy," in *Les Exégètes Syriaques: Actes du Colloque* XIII, *Patrimoine Syriaque*, ed. Paul Feghali (Lebanon: CERO, 2015): 1–27.

———, *Types and Symbols of the Church in the Writings of Jacob of Sarug* (Bavaria, diss., 2017).

P. M. Forness, "Cultural Exchange and Scholarship on Eastern Christianity. An Early Modern Debate over Jacob of Serugh's Christology," *JEasternCS* 70 (2018): 257–84.

———, *Preaching Christology in the Roman Near East: a Study of Jacob of Serugh* (Oxford University Press, 2018).

G. Friedlander (tr.), *Pirke de Rabbi Eliezer. The Chapters of Rabbi Eliezer the Great* (New York: Sepher-Hermon Press, 1981, 4th ed.).

A. Golitzin, "The Image and Glory of God in Jacob of Serug's Homily, *On the Chariot that Ezekiel the Prophet Saw*," *SVTQ* 47 (2003): 323–64.

———, "The Place of the Presence of God: Aphrahat of Persia's Portrait of the Christian Holy Man," in Simonos Petras Monastery (ed.) *Synaxis Eucharistiae. Charisteria eis timen Gerontos Aimilianou* (Athens: Indiktos Press, 2003), 397–447.

S. H. Griffith, "The Image of the Image Maker in the Poetry of St. Ephraem the Syrian," *StPatr* 25 (1993): 258–69.

M. Hansbury, "*Insight Without Sight*: Wonder as an Aspect of Revelation in the Discourses of Isaac the Syrian," *JCSSS* 8 (2008): 60–73.

———, "Love as an Exegetical Principle in Jacob of Serug," *Harp* XXVII (2011): 353–68.

———, "Patterns of Divine Mercy in Jacob of Serug and Isaac the Syrian," *PdO* 43 (2017) 195–211.

A. Harrak (tr.), "Memra 33 of Narsai: The Sacramental Nature of the 'Church of the Nations'," *PdO* 41 (2015): 181–203.

T. Jansma, "The Credo of Jacob of Serugh," *NAKG* 44 (1960): 18–36.

S. K. Joshua, *Church as the Bride of Christ, a Unique Divine-Human Relationship Model: A Study Based on the Select Homilies of Mar Jacob of Serug (451–521)*, (Bangalore diss., 2015).

S. A. Kaufman, tr. and Introd. *Jacob of Serug's Homilies on Elisha* (Gorgias Press, 2010).

G. A. Kiraz (ed.) *Jacob of Serugh and His Times* (Gorgias Press, 2010).

J. Kollamparampil, "Divine Pedagogy on the Road of Salvation and Early Syriac Perspectives," *PdO* 36 (2011): 85–98.

———, *Jacob of Serugh, Select Festal Homiles* (Bangalore: Dharmaram Publications, 1997).

———, *Salvation in Christ According to Jacob of Serug* (Bangalore: Dharmaram Publications, 2001).

J. Konat, "Christological Insights in Jacob of Seruh's Typology as Reflected in his *memre*," *ETL* 77 (2002): 46–72.

———, "A Metrical Homily of Jacob of Serugh on the Mysteries, Types, and Figures of Christ: Authentic or Compilation," *LM* 118 (2005): 71–86.

———, *The Old Testament Types of Christ as Reflected in the Select Metrical Homilies (memrē) of Jacob of Serugh* (Diss. Louvain, 1999).

———, "Typological Exegesis in the Metrical Homilies of Jacob of Serugh," *PdO* 31 (2006) 109–121.

———, "Typological Terminology of Jacob of Serugh," *Harp* (2005), 289–296.

T. Koonammakkal, *The Church in the Churches: A Syriac Ecclesiology* (Kuravilangad/Sleeva, 2118).

———, "The Self-Revealing God and Man in Ephrem," *Harp* VI 3 (1993), 233–248.

———, *The Theology of Divine Names in the Genuine Works of Ephrem*, Mōrān 'Eth'ō 40 (Kottayam: SEERI, 2015).

E. G. Mathews and J.P. Amar (tr.), *St. Ephrem the Syrian. Selected Prose Works* (Catholic University Press, 1994).

C. McCarthy (tr.), *Saint Ephrem's Commentary on Tatian's Diatessaron* (Oxford University Press, 1993).

R. Murray, *Symbols of Church and Kingdom* (Cambridge University Press, 1975); Rev. ed. (Piscataway, NJ: Gorgias Press, 2004).

———, "The Lance Which Reopened Paradise: A Mysterious Reading in the Early Syriac Fathers," *OCP* 39 (1973): 224–34.

———, "The Theory of Symbolism in St. Ephrem's Theology," *PdO* 6–7 (1975–76): 1–20.

J. Neusner, *The Incarnation of God.* The Character of Divinity in Formative Judaism, (Scholars Press Atlanta, Georgia 1992).

———, *Symbol and Theology in Early Judaism* (Fortress Press, 1991).

G. Olinder, *Iacobi Sarugenseis Epistulae quotquot supersunt*, *CSCO* II.45; *SS* 57; 1937.

J. Puthuparampil OIC, *Mariological Thought of Mar Jacob of Serugh* (451–521) Mōrān 'Eth'ō (Kottayam : SEERI, 2005).

E. Riad, *Studies in the Syriac Preface* (Stockholm: Almquist & Wiksell, 1988).

F. Rilliet, *Jacques de Saroug. Six Homélies Festales en Prose*, PO 196 (Brepols, 1986).

———, "La Louange des pierres et le tonnerre (Lk.19:40) chez Jacques de Saroug et dans la patristique syriaque," *RTP* 117 (1985): 293–304.

———, "La métaphore du chemin dans la sotériologie de Jacques de Saroug," *StPatr* 25 (1993), 324–31.

———, "Une Victime du Tournant des Études du Syriaques a la Fin du XIXe Siècle. Retrospective sur Jacques de Saroug dans la Science Occidentale," *ARAM*, 5 (1993), 465–480.

P. Schäfer, *The Hidden and Manifest God.* Some Major Themes in Early Jewish Mysticism (New York: State University Press).

G. Scholem, *Major Trends in Jewish Mysticism* (New York: Schocken Books, 1941).

E. E. Urbach, *The Sages: Their Concepts and Their Beliefs*, I. Abrahams (tr.) (Jerusalem: Hebrew University, 1979).

R. A. Darling Young, "The 'Church from the Nations' in the Exegesis of Ephrem," *OCA* 229 (1987): 111–121.

INDEX

References are to line numbers.

BIBLICAL REFERENCES

Genesis		15:19	256
28:18	13	16:1	272
Exodus		16:2–3	436
17:6	267	16:3	300, 330
Joshua		16:5ff	338
10:12	20	16:7	348
Judges		16:11	356
6:36–40	21	16:13	368
7:11	22	16:17	384
11:34–39	23	16:21	415, 419
13:5	40	16:23	435
13:7	51	16:25	440
13:9ff	48	1 Samuel	
13:14	50, 52	5:2–7	436
13:20	54, 68	Psalm	
14:5	82	80:5(LXX)	15
14:6	101-2	118:103	169
14:8	127	146:3	477
14:14	130, 133	John 5:31	424
14:15ff	186	6:33–5	154
15:4-5	201	8:44	95
15:5	215	Hebrews	
15:9, 10	231	11:32	36
15:11, 12	233		
15:15	237		

INDEX OF NAMES

Adam Aaron   17   Abraham 12

Adam 395, 399
Church 122
Church of Light 107
Church of the Nations 24, 114
Cross 117
Dagon 436
Daughter of the gentiles 109
Daughter of the pagans (Aramaeans) 91
Death 115, 151
Delilah 400, 403
Egypt 15
Eve 395, 399, 403
Gideon 21
Golgotha 13
Hebrew 97, 123, 149, 231, 308, 323, 440
Hebron 330
Isaac 13
Israel 40
Jephthah 23
Joseph 15
Joshua 19
Last Judgment 289
Manoah 62, 68
Midianites 22
Moses 16, 267

Nazirite 31, 38, 44, 51, 94, 99, 1321, 235, 279, 328, 359, 381, 384, 397, 400, 407, 411, 427, 446, 463, 471
Noah 11
Nun 19
Paradise 399
Paul 35
Philistines 75, 77, 89, 111, 135, 143, 149, 182, 184, 186, 198, 207, 229, 234, 239, 245, 319, 325, 328, 372, 386, 398, 415, 420, 437, 450, 467, 481
Samson 25, 36, 48, 62, 72, 83, 85, 89, 94-5, 98, 112, 116, 129, 139, 145, 157, 161, 167, 171, 183, 187, 194, 201, 227, 230, 232, 243, 250, 253, 255, 258, 263, 265, 270, 271, 273, 283, 291, 312, 315, 320, 328, 378, 395, 400, 402, 407, 431, 433, 436, 438, 441, 443, 463, 469, 478, 485
Seth 11
Sheol 309, 314, 316, 321
Sinai 16